LIBERTY
AND THE
WALL

of Separation Between Church and State

LIBERTY AND THE WALL

of Separation Between Church and State

Robert J. O'Keefe

Primix Publishing
East Brunswick Office Evolution
1 Tower Center Boulevard, Ste 1510
East Brunswick, NJ 08816
www.primixpublishing.com
Phone: 1-800-538-5788

© 2026 Robert J. O'Keefe . All rights reserved.

No part of this book may be reproduced, stored in a retrieval system, or transmitted by any means without the written permission of the author.

Published by Primix Publishing: 02/03/2026

ISBN: 979-8-89194-610-1(sc)
ISBN: 979-8-89194-611-8(hc)
ISBN: 979-8-89194-612-5(e)

Library of Congress Control Number: 2026902016

Any people depicted in stock imagery provided by iStock are models, and such images are being used for illustrative purposes only.

Certain stock imagery © iStock.

Because of the dynamic nature of the Internet, any web addresses or links contained in this book may have changed since publication and may no longer be valid. The views expressed in this work are solely those of the author and do not necessarily reflect the views of the publisher, and the publisher hereby disclaims any responsibility for them.

When a land transgresses it has many rulers; but with men of understanding and knowledge, its stability will long continue.
—Proverbs 28:2, RSV

Religion, morality, and knowledge, being necessary to good government and the happiness of mankind, schools and the means of education shall forever be encouraged.
—Northwest Ordinance of 1789

Contents

Preface ix
Introduction : A Religiously Neutral Education? xiii
Chapter 1 : Liberty 1
Chapter 2 : Debates 17
    Lincoln vs. Douglas 17
    Federalist vs. Anti-Federalist 29
    Federalist vs. Anti-Federalist II: Judicial Review 45
Chapter 3 : The Wall 57
Chapter 4 : Truth, That Which Corresponds to Reality 86
Chapter 5 : Freedom In A Godless World 114
Chapter 6 : Liberty Revisited 130
Chapter 7 : Writing on the Wall 144
Appendix A : Utopoan ideologies 148
Appendix B : Natural Law and Natural Right 157
Appendix C : To What May Be Attributed the Increase
               and Expansion of Christianity? 162
Notes 167
Bibliography 185

Preface

Founders of the United States repeatedly stressed the point that the virtue associated with religion is necessary for good government and liberty. That view seems to have been common enough in the late eighteenth century that no further explanation or justification was felt necessary. The founders expressed but did not argue. At the founding, the Establishment and Free Exercise clauses of the First Amendment, along with the associated concept of separation between church and state, were seen as necessary to keep the institutions of government and religion out of each other's pockets and meeting rooms. But separation was never thought to be a measure to prevent the role of religion in upholding virtue and morality in the functioning of government. The influence of denominational Christianity over public affairs was, at least in ceremony, evident and accepted. It hardly needed to be defended. Did President Washington not, at the behest of Congress, proclaim November 26, 1789, a day of thanksgiving to Almighty God immediately following Congress's approval of the First Amendment? Now, even the possibility that Christianity might exert influence over public matters is held in contempt. The point is perhaps best appreciated in that nowadays public virtue nearly seems to begin and end in a hesitancy to insert one's religious beliefs and values into the political process. All religion and its associated moralities, it is assumed, must be removed from governance; the separation between church and state must be total for the cause of liberty. The question now is, can the founders' view even be defended at all?

We would have to begin by asking if there ever was a link between Christianity and liberty, particularly, liberty of the American kind, which is our chief interest here. Today, it would seem that if there ever was a link, it is now so tenuous and feeble that it is not worth investigating. Present appearances to the contrary, it might be a case of a structure having been built and the builder having some time ago departed, leaving no signature. Denial of the builder's identity does not preclude making practical use of the structure. The founders were aware of the builder's identity. Some of the most influential of them believed the structure, the understanding of reality wrought by Christianity, was essential for the cause of liberty. This book exists because that understanding of reality and the platform it supplies to political liberty have more defenses than perhaps the founders were aware. That understanding will never be reclaimed unless taught, formally taught in church schools. Certainly, none other than churches are interested in churches regaining the slightest cultural authority. And rarely is anyone going to learn about and apply subjects weighed down by intellectual content without having been taught. The prerequisites of liberty have intellectual content. You do not need to look further than the Federalist Papers to find it. Moreover, the platform of liberty cannot be rediscovered or reinvented by every generation and still thrive. The subject needs to be formally taught.

Irrespective of whether Christianity had any involvement, that the subject of good government and liberty needs recovery from time to time is conspicuous. Today, the divide over what liberty consists of and requires seems unbridgeable. Each side fears that their liberty and rights are being taken away by the other. By winning over elections, legislation, and court rulings, contenders imagine they are reforming the thinking of their political adversaries. The tactic is a symptom of the vastness of the chasm in understanding. Reasoned arguments become ineffective. Instead, slogans are blasted and chants are hurled, not to persuade but to destroy the enemy. The point of stasis—that is, agreement on the root issue and its ramifications—is absent. The condition is paradoxical because it is only the prevalence of reasoned persuasion over coercion that identifies liberty in the first place. Coercion is liberty's devil. If reasoned argument is already ineffective in these matters, then liberty is already evaporating in the midst of volatility over how to achieve and maintain it.

It is necessary to steer around church-state conflicts over religious symbols, speech, and practices on public property and in public institutions. If the Grinch steals away the symbols and externalities of Christmas while yet unable to budge its spirit in the heart, others, thinking to banish the symbols and speech of Christianity, are likewise powerless against its truth. There is something more worthy of the church-state separation discourse: the nature of the good/evil polarity and the effect on liberty should its control fall into the wrong hands. The intent of this book is to show how and why the founders' view is justified and necessary.

Introduction

A Religiously Neutral Education?

Ideas about what liberty is and how to achieve and maintain it diverge greatly. First, there is an easy idea about liberty and a not-so-easy idea. The easy idea is that liberty is achieved by removing outdated moral boundaries and leveling the economic landscape so that everyone is free to do as they please and be happy. The not-so-easy idea is that liberty is earned by keeping the boundaries and ordering them according to timeless principles. The easy idea seems at once obvious. The not-so-easy or hard idea is not so obvious because boundaries, even if principled, do not, on the face of it, seem congruent with liberty. The hard idea requires finding, defending, and deferring to principles that are attached to something that transcends individuals and governments, something that no one can manipulate to their advantage. The easy idea produces a public realm that is mediated by political power, loudness, manipulation, deceit, trickery, treachery, and violence. The hard idea produces a public realm where at least opportunity exists for reasoned appeal in resolving conflicts over matters of public interest.

Some of the population wants to charge ahead and refashion government according to what they see as superior ideals. They are angry from seeing progress continually snagged on supposed self-evident propositions about political systems, burdened as they are by so many antiquated checks and balances that should have been cast off a hundred years ago. They believe that much of the American constitutional heritage and tradition of limited government is obsolete and irrelevant. Change is necessary to bring about greater collective good, specifically greater equality and diversity. They have faith in the possibility of benevolent democracy and that government can and should be *the* force for both change and good. A few of these are aware of their advantage, that those who demand change own the initiative while conservation is inherently a defensive position. These few are also enthusiastically aware that the public education system is a chief tool which, over time, is able to reform the culture by continually molding the thought patterns of future generations.

Other persons want to retain the authority of the constitutional heritage, the authority that elevates individual sovereignty in matters of belief. They recognize that government is not always all that benevolent. Government is often the enemy of liberty; a divided, constrained government is best. They are skeptical about forcing change by means of government, believing that forced change should only proceed with a heavy dose of caution, if at all. They are aware that cultural refashioning that depends on increasing government scope and authority invariably leads to a loss of liberty and is irreversible. Moreover, they see utopian visions with an emphasis on equality and greater collective good as generally containing faulty assumptions about human nature. They question whether everyone would really be satisfied with enforced equality and some activist's ideas about good. But they do at least share awareness with the other side. Seeing their influence slip away, they are grimly aware that public education is a chief tool, which, over time, is able to continually mold thought patterns of future generations.

A work associate once remarked to me that he lives in a small town with his wife and children where everyone pretty much knows everyone else. He went on to explain that the public school system is good and that he even sees some of his children's teachers in church. The suggestion here is, of course, that if the teachers are in church, they hold the same views about the world as he does, and there is little to worry about regarding the children's education. Nevertheless, there is school and then there is church, and not everything that may be taught in one may be taught in the other. The children's teachers could probably teach almost everything at church that they teach at school, but not everything at school that they would teach at church. At school, they are censored from teaching anything that would be regarded as a subject of particular interest at church. The immediate answer behind the censoring is the wall of separation between church and state, public schools being within the domain of state.

It is said that the metaphor of a wall separating church and state is written into the Constitution. The government cannot establish religious beliefs by, among other things, teaching them in the schools it runs. Behind the prohibition is the idea that everyone has a right to determine one's own religious belief and also a right not to be force-fed a belief with which one might disagree, especially by the state. The government cannot decide to abridge this right and other similar rights of self-determination. But if one were to ask, "Then who or what decides that such rights should exist?" the Declaration of Independence answers that all are endowed with them by their capital *C*—Creator.

Now the Creator is most certainly a church subject impermissible in government schools. It may seem somewhat incongruous then that the very right secured by the separation should prohibit any teaching about the basis of rights in the first place. Not wanting to call attention to this incongruity, other reasons are put forward as to why church subjects should be prohibited in schools: the perception of the nature of church and religion. Church and religion is the domain of faith and values, not that of the rationally defensible, it is said. The common perception is that differing beliefs and values are not able to be mediated by reason. The domain of faith and values, being subjective, cannot be verified as having true content as in the fashion of, say, science. Facts and reasoning, particularly scientific facts and reasoning, are objective. They are public resources. Beliefs and values are not and must be kept private and out of public education on that basis, as well as the wall of separation basis. Neutrality is the idealized position here; you are not supposed to impose your beliefs and values on someone else. Conversely, facts and science are okay to be imposed and, in fact, ought to be imposed.

But the question does not go away: what happens to liberty and individual rights if the Declaration of Independence's platform for them is void? It would seem that governments, which are often looking for ways to increase their command, would favor having authority over individual rights. It would mean that *they* get to bestow (and take back) rights. Who or what would say they could not? And would not extolling in its schools the benevolence of a government that grants many rights be the best way to get its citizens to go along with the idea? The Creator would not even have to be denied; the difference between an atheistic position (God does not exist) and a secular position (God may exist, but that existence is irrelevant) is of no practical significance.

Education that misinforms students about the basis and nature of reality and of humanity, or that neglects the means of attaining such knowledge, is failed education and a disservice. Beliefs and values have a strange tenacity by the very *fact* of their continuing existence. They cannot be eradicated. The value of individual liberty to pursue happiness, for example, is real. Faith in the democratic process is real. A faithless, valueless, religiously neutral education that admits only facts may be an impossibility. So perhaps the goal should be truthfulness rather than feigned neutrality. The honesty and relevance of education by the state may be questioned, and there are other options.

Is there a reason why, in the United States, there is mostly immigration and rarely emigration? Why would anyone want to move here? What is wrong with their own country that they would go through the trouble of such a major transplant out of familiar customs, relations, and language? Maybe there is a reason. It is not often that an accommodation of liberty, such as found here, just happens to pop up from time to time and from place to place as if any government or civilization could produce it. Political philosophies governing at other times and places have not generally shown accommodation. Therefore, it should be necessary to pay particular attention to that which does. The Declaration of Independence refers to an equal endowment of rights by the Creator as being self-evident truth. If there is a link between God and liberty, even perhaps between church and state, then there may be a threat to liberty. The self-evident truth of a creator is not as self-evident as when the Declaration of Independence was written.

CHAPTER 1

LIBERTY

In other countries, the people, more simple, and of a less mercurial cast, judge of an ill principle in government only by an actual grievance; here they anticipate the evil, and judge of the pressure of the grievance by the badness of the principle. They augur misgovernment at a distance, and sniff the approach of tyranny in every tainted breeze.
—Edmund Burke[1]

With no pretense to being comprehensive, there are a few elements that would seem, from experience, to be essential to liberty as it is enjoyed in the United States. The most obvious and most endeared of these, at least by some, could only be the Constitution.

The Constitution

It had not been a frequent occurrence in history to see a nation debating and deliberating over the sort of government they should have. In fact, in the entire history of the world to 1787, it is doubtful that anyone had ever seen ordinary citizens engaged in a debate on what form of government they should have—not in imagination, in reality. A national government was being established not by "accident and force," as Alexander Hamilton wrote in Federalist 1, but upon "reflection and choice." To see this actually happening was nothing short of astonishing. But that is what was taking place during the 1787–88 ratifying conventions in each of the thirteen states as representatives in convention, chosen by the people of each state, considered whether (what at that time was) the proposed constitution should replace the Articles of Confederation and Perpetual Union.

Representatives of twelve of the thirteen states had met in Philadelphia all during the previous summer upon what had become a clean slate. What they were proposing, if accepted, would transform the national government's purpose, its organization, its procedures, its limits of authority, and how its representatives and top offices would be staffed through elections. This had been a tedious balancing exercise. How was it possible to secure the rights and liberties of individual citizens and of the states while, at the same time, granting the national government the authority and dispatch necessary to fulfill essential functions that it was not empowered to perform under the Articles of Confederation? There was a need to bring the independent states, jealous of their newly won liberty, into alignment not only to suppress their mutual enmities but to make the nation appear as one in the eyes of the world. This required a government with much more authority than the Articles of Confederation had permitted. The worry was over the corruptibility of human nature, especially the corruptibility of governing officials who, when handed authority, invariably tend to exhibit more enthusiasm in the use of that authority than restraint and, more often than not, to the general detriment of liberty. So it was necessary for the citizens and the thirteen states not only to empower their national government but to also govern that government, lest their liberty evaporate.

The mechanisms being proposed to govern the government were, in essence, three. First, there would be a separation into legislative, executive, and judicial departments or branches. The making of laws, the enforcing of laws, and the deciding of cases under the laws would thereby operate under separate leadership.[2]

- Members of the House of Representatives, the first house of the legislative branch, would represent the people most directly. A representative would be chosen by popular vote in each congressional district every two years.

- In the second house of the legislature, the Senate, each state's two senators would be chosen by that state's legislature for staggered six-year terms at either a two-or four-year interval. The Senate would, thereby, represent the states.
- The executive or president would be chosen every four years by electors of all the states based on the popular vote in each state—the number of each state's electors being the number of its senators and representatives.
- Supreme Court justices and other federal judges would, according to Article II, Section 2, be appointed for life terms by the president "with the Advice and Consent of the Senate."

Diversity in the nature of the branches and their dissimilar assigned oversights would *intentionally* make agreement among the branches on government policies and laws more difficult to achieve. Each branch would further retain certain specified constitutional means of thwarting the purposes of the other branches so as to be able to stop the other branches from fulfilling their goals. Under this three-branch and bicameral legislative arrangement, it was anticipated that any proposed legislation or policy would have to be generally well aligned with the overall public will for some time before it could become law and enforced.

Then there were restrictions to be imposed on the national government. In Article I, Section 8, and certain provisions in articles III and IV, the legislative agenda was to be limited to a specific slate of matters—taxation, immigration and naturalization, regulation of commerce, coining of money, copyrights and patents, provision for federal courts subordinate to the supreme court, jurisdiction of the supreme and federal courts, provision for armed forces, declarations of war, definitions of felonies and associated punishments, admission of new states, the governance of territories, and little else. In Article I, Section 9, specific prohibitions on the legislature were to be imposed including prohibitions on passing ex post facto laws (laws directing penalties against acts previous to the law's passage), taxes on exports from any state, laws preferential to one state over another, and the granting of titles of nobility. The executive and judicial branches, according to the proper nature of their roles, could not surpass what the legislature was authorized to do. As a further check on the national government, at least in theory, the state governments, in guarding their domains of authority, would prune any attempt by the national government to outgrow its constitutional box.

It was necessary for the people themselves to have a role in their government, though not too directly or closely. The people needed to be separated from direct democratic rule, lest a majority of them similarly exhibit too much enthusiasm in the use of majority power. It is an empirical fact in the history of democratic governments—a majority, once swept along by some transient discontent or fashion, invariably tramples the liberties and rights of minorities. As paradoxical as it appears, with their right to self-government so coveted in the Revolution and now well guarded, the people themselves had to be somewhat quarantined from the legislative process. To the end, then, of preventing democratic excesses, the proposed constitution specified forms of representation in the legislative branch. Decision-making was thereby to be removed from direct citizen participation. Representation would prevent the people from wielding direct control over the government, and perhaps as importantly, representatives in assembly would provide a forum for debate and deliberation, something that the people as a whole could never do. The people, nevertheless, had to have a voice, and a system of periodically refreshed representation was found to be as able a fix for that necessity as could be found. The proposed constitution thus codified barriers and a mesh-work of sorts that would work to confound the tendency of both rulers and democratic majorities to turn despotic.

In its separations, limitations, and forms of representation, the proposed constitution was going to be an experiment. Such a written constitution specifying how a national government was to be organized and operated, and what it could do and what it would be prevented from doing, had not been attempted before. While it leaned heavily on the wisdom of some of the greatest political minds in history to that point, there was a substantial dose of new thinking mixed in. The initiative still is an experiment. It is an experiment to see if liberty can be sustained in the face of ever-present threats against it. Besides the danger of foreign invasion, there are constant internal dangers— the tendency of rulers to exercise more control than authorized, the tendency of majorities to trample over minorities, and the tendency of citizens in their individual pursuits of happiness to encroach upon the like pursuits of others. Decisions and policies on myriads of particular and temporal matters of public interest require continual resolution between governmental exercise of power and individual liberty and rights. It is an ongoing test to see if the Constitution's form and function are adequate to permit governmental latitude in dealing decisively with public matters while simultaneously resisting encroachments against the liberty of the citizens and of the states. The authors' wisdom remains alive today as one considers that human nature and the problems of governance by corruptible men are no different today than they were yesterday.

The success of the Constitution toward the mission of governing a government—emphatically not its people or the separate states—may be measured by comparison to the liberty or, more accurately, the lack of it in other times and places. The 1787 Constitution, along with the 1776 Declaration of Independence and the 1789 Bill of Rights, are, therefore, worthy of study. Yet the wisdom contained in these charters, the wisdom necessary to order the foundation of liberty, is not at all obvious from a casual reading. The best way to begin to understand and appreciate that wisdom is to revisit the debate that took place at the time the Constitution was being ratified. That debate is introduced in the next chapter. There were good reasons for wanting to argue for ratification, reasons that remain relevant today. But there were also good reasons for wanting to thwart ratification, reasons that also remain relevant today.

The Great Inversion

Constitutional principles of separation, limitation, and representation did not just suddenly pop into existence. It would be inexcusable not to credit earlier developments in the quest for government attuned to liberty. There were circumstances and trends beforehand that made it possible, if not likely. One of these is that King John of England found, in the year 1215, that, even as the king, he could not do as he pleased in every matter. He was going to have to be subject to certain resolutions. The resolutions he was going to have to be subject to were those laid down by the English barons who stood against him in arms on the plain of Runnymede by the River Thames. The collection of resolutions or articles became known as the Great Charter, the Magna Carta. The chief significance of this charter was the idea that laws should rule over even the king, a radical departure from the standard practice of kings being above the law.[3] The rule of law meant that both government and the governed would be under law—the same law.[4]

By the end of the thirteenth century, the assembly of English barons, to which were added higher clergy and prominent townspeople, was formally called *Parliament*. Besides determinations of law and the means by which members would advise the king, the king had to appeal to Parliament for revenue, that is taxes. Parliament was taxation with representation. Parliamentary authority over the king was clumsily and recklessly asserted when Parliament convened the High Court of Justice to try King Charles I in 1649. When the court had finished its business, the lord president of the court, John Bradshaw, ordered sentence to be pronounced against the king. The unfortunate Charles was executed shortly thereafter. In 1688, parliamentary authority over the king was more prudently and wisely established when the new king William of Orange did not assume the throne by virtue of a line of hereditary descent as was customary but was, instead, appointed by Parliament to replace James II. This event is known by historians as England's Glorious Revolution. These two balance of power developments, the Magna Carta and parliamentary authority over kings, however, were out-of-the-ordinary trajectories. Other countries were not as fortunate.

The quest for political liberty from overlording kings was accompanied by quests for religious liberty from overlording religion. From 1517, the Protestant Reformation began to throw open the door to alternate forms of Christianity in Western Europe and the idea that people could follow their own understanding of the Bible rather than that of a church hierarchy claiming to be the universal church. But here was a case of too much reform proceeding too quickly. The Reformation produced much religious confusion and conflict, and freedom of conscience saw little progress. A subject found holding a religious belief contrary to that of the king was still taken as rebellion, and rebellions, armed or otherwise, were suppressed. Murder and mayhem persisted in European wars of religion from soon after 1517 until the treaty of 1648. Any non-state sanctioned religious beliefs were continually under threat of persecution and prosecution by official church-state governance. The religion of the people remained the religion of the ruler.

The oppressive situation stirred certain disfavored religious groups to set up their own church-state operations in New England beginning in 1620 with Separatist Pilgrims, followed by Puritans in 1630. In this, the colonial period in North America was not entirely free of church-state overlording. As in the Old World, there was ill-treatment toward those who would not comply with the local church-state alliance. The contrast was that in the New World, church-state interests were not intensified by political and economic agendas.

Church-state interrelation also began to track a different trajectory in North America. Here, there was a certain fortuitous characteristic that Europe did not enjoy: much not-already-owned, non-jurisdictional land. The abundance of North American land was such that religious dissent could not be contained. Dissenters could and did move outside the perimeters of the Massachusetts Bay's church-state colony. Initially, Rhode Island became a haven for New England's religious dissenters. Later, in 1684, Pennsylvania was founded upon a policy of religious toleration where any religion was accepted. Other disfavored religious groups, Quakers and Baptists, saw fit to migrate over from the Old World. At the same time, the land supplied economic opportunity, a relief from the European absence of not-already-owned land. Outside of New England, other colonies began as government-authorized business ventures to draw wealth in one way or another from the land and from trade—Virginia, New York, New Jersey, Maryland, Delaware, Carolina, and Georgia.

For nearly a century and a half, the North American colonies continued, remote and insignificant to the mind of the home government in England. Even with the favorable trade winds, it took more than a month to get from one side of the Atlantic to the other. The colonies had to solve their own problems and manage their own affairs.[5] Parliament only exercised taxation authority over the colonies' overseas trade. But the colonies prospered, and rival interests of empire began to dispute over control of the continent and its trade. War with France followed, the Seven Years' War (also known as the French and Indian War). England prevailed in this war, acquiring control of all eastern North America at the war's end in 1763. In 1764, Parliament began to eye the colonies' internal commerce to tax it. They needed to service the debt England had incurred during the war. The authority to tax anything was the authority that Parliament assumed all along, only having not seen a necessity to exercise that before. But there was a problem. The colonies were too long accustomed to attending to their own taxation. To now forfeit that independence, even if achieved under the happenstance of colonial circumstances, registered poorly.

The indignant colonists scrambled to come up with a political theory that would justify their continued autonomy and denial of parliamentary rule. What they settled on was the idea of English philosopher John Locke (one of the most sensible of philosophers) that the only proper authorization of government was the peoples' consent.[6] Sovereignty, here defined as the source or seat of political power, was to be recognized as positioned within the people collectively as opposed to being positioned in a king or a representative assembly such as Parliament. So if there were to be taxes, they would be levied by the colonists' own governments, not by a far-off legislature whom they had never consented to tax them. The position was backed by the Magna Carta's provision against taxation without representation and the fact that the colonists had not been invited to send representatives to Parliament. Parliamentary legislation could not contravene the natural rights of Englishmen, which, not having been dispensed by legislation, could not be taken away by legislation. Separatist colonial churches joined the protest against parliamentary rule. There was apprehension that the Church of England might follow the lead of parliamentary authority and begin to assert itself as the religious authority in the colonies as it did in England. That anxiety paralleled the indignation and resistance of the colonial legislative assemblies against parliamentary taxation of the colonies' internal commerce.[7]

On one side of the Atlantic was the claim of sovereignty of the people, the colonists, and the necessity of their consent. On the other was the increased attention of the home government to the profitability of its North American "plantations." A collision of interests was inevitable. By 1775, that collision had become violent. The supplanting of parliamentary authority with the peoples' authority necessitated an instrument by which the people would justify such authority, and in 1776, that instrument materialized as the Declaration of Independence. Familiar passages in the Declaration express well this revolution in political thought: "That to secure these [natural] rights, Governments are instituted among Men, deriving their just powers from consent of governed" and "That whenever any Form of Government becomes destructive of these ends, it is the Right of the People to alter or to abolish it, and to institute new Government." In these words, the sole purpose of government, to secure the rights of the governed, is asserted, and the basis of its authority, the consent of the governed, is confirmed. The American Revolution, with the aid of the colonists' former enemy, France, achieved victory at Yorktown, Virginia, and independence from England in 1781.

The new Constitution, proposed in 1787 and ratified in 1788, became the people's expression of their authority or, as stated in Article VI, "the supreme Law of the Land." "We the People… " begins the Constitution's preamble in oversized letters. That, according to its authors, was the first necessary entry in the formula for liberty. The collective authority of the people is what gives the Constitution its authority. It is how the people tell the government what it can and cannot do and how to do what it is to do. Those who would presume to rule were thereby, in turn, to be ruled.

Thus, over the centuries, the traditional hierarchy of authority in Western civilization was stood on its head. Instead of king over people, it was now legislature over king (no longer called king but executive or president), written constitution over legislature, and people over constitution. The government was ordered and confined by boundaries and stipulations of a constitution set in place by the people. Only the people acting collectively through their states could alter the constitution; the national government could not alter it. This inversion—government restrained by law and law established under the authority of the people—was an innovation ripe for just this point in history, a point toward the end of what historians refer to as the Enlightenment era. This was the period roughly coincident with the eighteenth century, beginning with England's Glorious Revolution of 1688 and ending with the French Revolution in the 1790s. The Enlightenment era had, in its contempt of the hierarchical authority of kings and bishops and its elevation of reason, handed down sovereignty of the people and governance under their consent. The Enlightenment also further cemented the concepts of equality under law and unalienable rights. Principles of liberty and of government superior to these have not yet been found and likely never will.

No Grand Utopian Ideals

How well can a governing authority secure and maintain itself while allowing alternate political views to be voiced and heard within its domain? To what degree can a government permit the free exchange of ideas, especially ideas that threaten its founding principles? It should be worthwhile to observe the extent to which liberties—particularly those of religion, speech, press, and peaceful assembly—are honored under the various governments of the world. Which of these most respect the right for views opposed to that which rules to be aired in public? The normal ascendance of governmental, self-preservational expediency over any other concern cannot be overstated. But if to the natural tendency to annihilate contrary views are added justifications from religion or some political philosophy, governments attain pinnacles of self-righteousness in their oppressions that would otherwise appear as just plain thuggery.

Likewise, it is well that in political environments that do honor the right for competing political views to be heard, one takes note of the degree to which reciprocity of that right would be granted by a competing political theory's practice. Would critics of the existing governing authority bear with the same degree of criticism against themselves if they were in power? Do they take advantage of present liberties to push their ideologies—liberties they themselves would never reciprocate? Once in power, would they tolerate subversive activities similar to ones they themselves might instigate to gain control? It is well to note that the means by which some would acquire political rule also likely reflect the means by which they would sustain it.[8] If coercion, violence, and a cover of misinformation, for example, are characteristics of an attempt to gain political power, the same are likely to be characteristics of the manner in which it would be kept.

The measure of a political system's liberty is not only the degree to which there is freedom to dissent but also the degree to which dissent whose intent is to take away that liberty may be resisted. The American constitutional system has accommodated dissent and contained subversive activities without obliterating them while yet remaining reasonably secure. Recent attempts to subvert constitutional rule include the Soviet Communist Party infiltration of the federal government during the mid-twentieth century and the present Council on Foreign Relations globalist/socialist infiltration. Neither a communist nor a global socialist system, if the subversion of constitutional rule were to succeed, would ever reciprocate the same freedom to dissent. The appeal of such systems is the promise of an ideal or utopian society. But that promise is likely to come at the cost of freedom to oppose it.

The world has some experience now with utopian political theories. In this experience, it has been seen that all means necessary to achieve the ideal society have been justified by the ideal society. The success of the utopian theory or ideology is invariably more important than the individual. Achievement of collective goals and ideals requires government exercise of power to force individuals to comply with them. Individual pursuits of happiness are ruthlessly subordinated to the collective pursuit of the ideal. It has been seen that perpetual oppression, terror, and the perversion of justice are necessary to attain terminally elusive utopian goals. Public criticism cannot be tolerated. Dissenters are often kidnapped or murdered by the state. Political and religious activity is heavily regulated, and if it is not in accord precisely with the ruling ideology, it is stamped out. Utopian theories are unburdened by a realistic understanding of human nature, and in fact, they seek to redefine human nature for the greater glory of the state. (See Appendix A for further discussion of utopian ideologies.)

The governing system friendliest to liberty is, perhaps oddly, the one that has no utopian vision at all. No vision aptly describes the American constitutional system. The only grand ideal that the Constitution defends is that citizens are free to pursue their own grand ideals or none at all, if that should be their wish. It is not that there should not be any grand ideals or causes. It is only that the government is hindered from directing them. That, of course, means that the achievement of any grand ideal or cause must be a private initiative. As a private initiative, any participation in its pursuit would necessarily be voluntary, not compulsory. The voluntary nature of participation, in turn, means that its achievement must depend on reasoned or impassioned persuasion, not power and force. This point, once brought into awareness, is obvious in browsing the Constitution.

The Constitution is a rather sleepy read, even as short as it is. This is not intended as a derogatory remark. It means that the Constitution's wisdom is hidden from the casual reader—that wisdom being as much a matter of what is not there as what is there. Instead of setting forth some grand utopian vision or an ideal or model society, the Constitution only splits up and restrains government, putting it at the service of individual rights it did not grant. Unlike some pretended charters of liberty, such as the 1948 United Nations Universal Declaration of Human Rights, there is no pomposity about it. Rights of conscience, speech, press, assembly, arms, protection against unwarranted search or seizure, trial by jury, and others are considered as pre-existing. They *precede* the Constitution rather than being created or granted by it. The Constitution presumes only to bar the national government from abridging them. There is no veneration of economic, social, political, religious, or philosophical ideals to be found. While it may be necessary that some such ideals are present as a cohesive social force to hold a nation together, nothing of the sort is found in the Constitution. In fact, the Constitution does its best to arrange the organization and procedures of government so as to prevent the advocacy of any specific such ideal from taking control of the government.

Utopian goals and ideal societies are not realized by individuals pursuing their own interests. Utopian goals and protocols of ideal societies must be imposed. Individual self-interest must be subordinated to the collective interest and unchecked government invariably empowers itself to do that. Wherever and whenever government appropriates such power, good sense and experience attest it to be the end of individual liberty. It is because every governing system that involves some visionary utopian ideal invariably regards individuals as means, or worse, as obstacles to realizing that ideal. The violence and crudeness of the hatchet job necessary to achieve the utopian state always reveals its true nature. In contrast, the Constitution's emptiness with respect to such ideals and goals means that, at least in Constitutional theory, no one should become a means or an obstacle to some grand political end.

Appeal to a Higher Authority

The fact of the Declaration of Independence's reasoned appeal and the object of that appeal are made clear in these words: "A decent respect to the opinions of mankind requires that they [the people announcing their separation] should declare the causes which impel them to the separation" and "Appealing to the Supreme Judge of the world for the rectitude of our intentions… " There was, first, a reasoned appeal in the declaration of causes—the causes being the list of grievances that followed in the text of the Declaration. Then there was an appeal to the Supreme Judge. That appeal was made over and above the Parliament and king of Great Britain. An appeal *to* the king had already been tried by a petition called the Olive Branch Petition drafted in 1775 by John Dickinson (1732–1808) on behalf of the Continental Congress. This had failed. The king refused even to receive it. A recurrence of that appeal could never justify independence *from* Parliament and king. The authority of Great Britain over the colonies had to be nullified to justify independence. The only higher authority to which appeal could be made was to "the Supreme Judge of the world" and to "the Laws of Nature and of Nature's God," which, according to the Declaration's authors, was what entitled them to "assume among the powers of the earth, [a] separate and equal station."[9] Appeal over the head of power is the basis of the subordination of might to right. Once independence was achieved, however, there no longer was a need to retain an appeal of that sort, or was there?

The Constitution became, and is now, the authority to which any appeal regarding government is to be directed. But there can be matters over which the government is called to decide and to act on which the Constitution is silent or at least indeterminate, or that appeal to the Constitution is unable to resolve. What constitutes the proper boundaries of the citizens' own liberty or what rights are legitimate to claim and what if there is disagreement among the people? Sovereign entities that they are, citizens are accountable neither to other citizens nor to government for their beliefs, including beliefs about the proper boundaries of their own liberty and rights. Know for certain that the Constitution is aimed solely at the national government to restrain it, not the citizens (though Article I, Section 10 also imposes restrictions on the states). The Constitution imposes no injunctions or commandments on the people whatsoever. Its list of "thou shalts" and "thou shalt nots" applies to the government, not the people.

We can agree that liberty was and is the great prize in the most absolute sense. But the inherent tension between individual liberty, letting everyone believe and do as they wish, and public order and communal harmony, having everyone agree on and do what is right and just, must be resolved continually. One person's idea of good cannot be another's idea of evil without causing discord and turmoil. Is there some mechanism that automatically unites a people to agree on what is right and just without being compulsory? Well, in fact, there are no mechanisms, at least none in the Constitution. The lack of something that can reign in opinion about what is right, good, and just must inevitably result in conflicting exercise of rights, even a breakdown of justice. What are rights really, and who or what defines them? Or how are they discovered and agreed upon? What happens to liberty when rights, and the proper boundaries on them, are the subject of wrangling between mutually hostile interest groups?

It is needful to enjoy some consensus on the matter. A people divided in the sense of their own rights are vulnerable to having them aligned by force. Agreement on the proper boundaries of rights must be voluntary. Anyone attempting to align them by force would probably not have their preservation as a top concern.

The Declaration of Independence was, and might still be, the preeminent unifying consensus vehicle. Returning to it again, it is seen that the purpose of government is to secure the people's rights, a point evident from the sentence already quoted: "That to secure these rights, Governments are instituted among Men, deriving their just powers from the consent of the governed." Rights are thereby only to be secured by government; it has no authority over their determination. Here, the tables are turned on government, which heretofore was the most real threat against the people's liberty. Now it is supposed to defend and uphold them—quite a reversal of the usual practice as already elaborated. No one should be taking away what they never gave out in the first place. As to the rights themselves, recognition as to their origin is found in these often-referenced words appearing just prior to the above sentence in the Declaration: "We hold these truths to be self-evident, that all men are created equal, that they are endowed by their Creator with certain unalienable Rights." The people's rights are presumed to be Creator-endowed, not government-endowed. This is only minimally theocratic; the Declaration's earlier phrase "the Laws of Nature and of Nature's God" is its reference to natural law and natural right. (See Appendix B for an introduction to natural law and natural right.) The security associated with Creator-endowed rights begins with the understanding that they pre-exist government. In being thus Creator-based, they are fixed and irrevocable, unable to be redefined by any man or majority.

So is the Declaration's reference to the Creator a ritual formality or a reality? If it is only a ritual formality, liberty would seem to sit on rather hollow, even deceptive ground. It is certain that a Creator is not as self-evident a truth as it was in the past. Intellectual demands are heavy in an age of scientific naturalism. Though there is much to this question that will be covered in later chapters, for the moment, it is understood that the one authority that would qualify as incorruptible, in principle, is the Creator, if there is one.

By measure of the elements of liberty outlined in this chapter, a written Constitution aligned to the great inversion, with no grand causes or ideals except liberty itself, and stationed as the authority over government, the generation of 1787–88, did well in concluding their debates and deliberations. But there was more work to do. There was one controversy over what was right, good, and just that the Constitution did not and could not answer, and that was poised to shatter the achievement of all the objectives found in its preamble.

CHAPTER 2

Debates

Lincoln vs. Douglas

Throughout the years preceding the 1861–65 War Between the States, westward migration and settlement repeatedly provoked contention over the question of slavery. Should slavery be permitted in the Western territories, and in the new states formed from those territories, or not? And what effect would the answer to that have on the balance of power between slave and free states in the US Congress, particularly the Senate? A balance between slave and free states was viewed as essential to preserving the union. The threat of disunion should one section have the votes to routinely impose their will as to the slavery question on the other was real. But how long could such a balance be maintained?

But there was a bigger, more central question looming beneath the territorial provocation. In the words of Allen C. Guelzo, a historian of the Lincoln-Douglas debates commenting in reference to the slavery matter, "Did popular government exist merely to ratify the decisions of its majorities, no matter what those decisions were, or was democracy wedded to a set of fundamental propositions that those majorities were accountable to? And where did those propositions come from?"[1] Was every question to be decided by democratic majority, or were there some matters that were independent of majority opinion and could not be thus decided, and if so, how were they to be decided?

That was the question at the center of the Lincoln-Douglas debates. These debates have proven to be among the most momentous of oratorical events in United States history. We can draw a lesson from them in observing how certain principles were elevated and subsequently encoded in law, if not ingrained into popular thought.

Both the Declaration of Independence and the Constitution are very circumspect with regard to slavery; the term does not appear in either. In the Declaration of Independence, the right of "property" had to become "the pursuit of happiness." Otherwise, the Declaration would surely have been construed by the southern states to mean more than what the Continental Congress as a whole was prepared to give it. Slaves were regarded as property. The equality clause was set forth as a universal principle. The less said about slavery, the better. The Constitution's only references to slavery were in the mention of fugitive slaves as "persons held to service or labor" in Article IV, Section 2, and of the slave trade as the "migration or importation of such persons as any of the states now existing shall think proper to admit" in Article I, Section 9. A slave-based economy and culture had already been long entrenched in the American colonies by the late eighteenth century. To think that in the thick of the crises that led to these documents, it could be decreed out of existence by some pronouncement in them was utterly unrealistic. The abolition of slavery would set back or destroy much, if not all, of the economy of many of the southern states. It was understood that the southern states would not sign on to any constitutional agreement should the institution's continuity be threatened in any way.

Equally desired was to avoid its further establishment. Awareness of the hypocrisy of the colonists' quest for liberty from English oppression while they kidnapped, transported under appalling conditions, sold in markets, and then subjected to a permanent degrading imprisonment of so many hundreds of thousands was increasing. Patrick Henry (1736–99), for example, could not ignore the contradiction involved in maintaining slavery "at a time when the rights of humanity are defined and understood with precision in a country above all others fond of liberty."[2] The Northwest Ordinance of 1789, one of the first acts of the new congress, in renewing the 1787 act of the same name, reaffirmed the exclusion of slavery from the territory that would later become the states of Ohio, Michigan, Indiana, Illinois, and Wisconsin. Article I, Section 9 of the Constitution permitted Congress to abolish the slave trade in 1808, which they did not hesitate to do in 1807, declaring that trade illegal immediately upon the following January 1. These are clear indications that the founders, unable to effectively remove the practice, sought at least to contain it in the hope that it would eventually be found disadvantageous in some way and then abandoned.

Under the leadership of Kentucky Senator Henry Clay (1777–1852), the compromises of 1820 and 1850 achieved temporary respite between the North and South over the slavery question. Preservation of a status quo balance in the Senate was maintained as new states continued to be added to the union. The 1820 Missouri Compromise established, among several actions, the Missouri line at 36 degrees, 30 minutes north of which slavery was to be forever excluded. Missouri (north of the line) then promptly entered the union as a slave state balanced by Maine entering as a free state. The Compromise of 1850 likewise established a number of balancing measures, including the admission of California as a free state and a shoring up of fugitive slave laws.

But then the Kansas-Nebraska Act of 1854 swept these judiciously crafted compromise measures away. The Kansas-Nebraska Act was, under the circumstances, probably the most volatile piece of legislation in US history. The Act repealed the 1820 and 1850 compromise measures (it is noteworthy that the Act was initially worded to do that implicitly so as not to draw attention to the fact) and then introduced the idea of "popular sovereignty" into the Kansas and Nebraska territories. (Note that in 1854, Nebraska also included territory that was to become North Dakota and South Dakota.) Popular sovereignty meant that citizens of the territories would be permitted to decide for themselves whether their territorial governance and future state constitution were to be slave or free.

The Kansas-Nebraska Act was introduced under Illinois Democratic Party Senator Stephen A. Douglas's sponsorship as chairman of the Senate Committee on Territories. Douglas's intent with this legislation was to promote Western expansion through settlement and territorial development, continental integration via a first transcontinental railroad, and to promote economic development, especially in his own state of Illinois, being as it was along the central and northern routes to the Western territories, and most specifically Kansas and Nebraska.

Douglas (1813–61) championed the idea of popular sovereignty to help secure southern backing for the act. He thought it necessary to do this because in territory where slavery was excluded under the Missouri Compromise (i.e., Kansas and Nebraska), southern congressmen and senators, even members of his own party, were not otherwise interested in organizing any territorial government. The act was further an attempt to boot the contentious slavery question out of Congress. Douglas viewed popular sovereignty as an expedient gesture of little consequence because the climate and geography of this territory was, he thought, inhospitable to slave-based economies. But both in its practical implementation and in moral principle, it was a serious miscalculation. The aspect of the act that made it so explosive, and which Douglas failed to anticipate, was that neither the radical abolitionists nor the southern slave power would ever permit the question to be resolved by popular vote of a bunch of pioneers. The matter was too contentious for either faction to not attempt to steer the outcome. As much as Congress thus attempted to quietly place the conflict over slavery and its resolution outside of its walls with the Kansas-Nebraska Act, it could not. A pre-Civil War civil war erupted over the Kansas territory's status as slave or free in Kansas itself, and that conflict spilled back over into Congress as hot sectarian division raged over the terms of Kansas's admission as a state.

Into the provocation resulting from the Kansas-Nebraska Act stepped Abraham Lincoln (1809–65). Lincoln had left the United States Congress in 1849 after a single two-year term and had returned to his private law practice. But whatever urge there was to return to politics now had a conduit; he could not remain detached from a reopening of opportunity to extend the evils of slavery. Lincoln's Springfield and Peoria, Illinois, speeches of September and October 1854 began, among other arguments opposing the expansion of slavery into the territories, an appeal to the Declaration of Independence's equality clause: "We hold these truths to be self-evident that all men are created equal..." In these speeches, he stressed the incompatibility of slavery with the Declaration of Independence's principle of equality under law.

Lincoln did not propose to interfere in any manner with the constitutionally protected right of existing states to do as they pleased regarding the institution of slavery. His arguments applied exclusively to the territories, that slavery ought to be prevented only from expansion. The Kansas-Nebraska Act should be repealed, argued Lincoln, and the compromise measures restored. As Lincoln's Whig Party was disintegrating because of internal division over the question, he would shortly identify with the newly forming Republican Party. In 1856, that party's entire platform very nearly consisted solely of excluding slavery from the territories and admitting Kansas as a free state. The 1856 Republican Party Platform stated in part:

> Our republican fathers, when they had abolished slavery in all our national territory, ordained that no person should be deprived of life, liberty, or property, without due process of law. It becomes our duty to maintain this provision of the constitution against all attempts to violate it for the purpose of establishing slavery in any territory of the United States, by positive legislation prohibiting its existence or extension therein... We deny the authority of congress, of a territorial legislature, of any individual or association of individuals, to give legal existence to slavery in any territory of the United States, while the present constitution shall be maintained.[3]

If the Kansas-Nebraska Act was not already enough of a provocation, the Supreme Court's 1857 ruling in *Dred Scott v. Sanford* about pushed agitation over the edge. Dred Scott, a Missouri slave, had sued for his freedom after being taken by his owner into the state of Illinois and then to Minnesota (which was, at that time, part of the Wisconsin territory), both free areas, for some period of time. State and territorial law prohibited the holding of slaves, and so legally, Scott should have been set free. But the Court ruled that black persons were not citizens and thus could not sue (even though they were already citizens in some free states). "Not only could blacks not sue, slave property," said the Court, "was the same as any other property, and an owner could not be prohibited from transporting that into a territory." Chief Justice Roger Taney wrote the opinion of the Court stating:

> An act of congress which deprives a citizen of the United States of his liberty or property, merely because he came himself or brought his property into a particular Territory of the United States, and who had committed no offense against the laws, could hardly be dignified with the name of due process of law.

The practical result was that slavery could be extended to territories by court decree as the question was now reduced to one of property rights. Neither Congress nor territorial legislatures could prohibit slavery in the territories. Popular sovereignty was also effectively rendered void because no territory could exclude slave property from entering. The ruling had a potential to lead to legalization of slavery in northern free states as well.

In 1858, Douglas and Lincoln campaigned for the Illinois Senate seat held by Douglas. From August 21 through October 15, seven three-hour debates were held throughout Illinois, one in each congressional district of the state except in the Chicago and Springfield districts because both candidates had already given speeches there. A one-hour opening speech by the first candidate was followed by a one-and-a-half-hour rebuttal by his opponent, and then a half-hour rejoinder by the first, with the first speaker alternating between Douglas and Lincoln throughout the seven debates. Douglas, who was first elected by the Illinois legislature to the United States Senate in 1847, had since become the most powerful and influential senator in the country and remained immensely popular in Illinois. Yet because of national attention given to these debates, Lincoln, who was largely unknown outside of Illinois even as late as 1858, emerged as a growing threat not only to Douglas's reelection but to his political future and presidential prospects as well.

Lincoln's position in the debates was only this: He sought to restrict slavery from the territories while upholding the constitutional rights of slave owners in the states where it already existed. He opposed extension of slavery into territories because of the moral wrong and the incompatibility with the principles of the Declaration of Independence. He also foresaw that the balance of representation in Congress over the question could not be maintained indefinitely. Lincoln's June 1858 House Divided speech in Springfield, Illinois, is noteworthy:

> A house divided against itself cannot stand. I believe this government cannot endure permanently half slave and half free. I do not expect the union to be dissolved. I do not expect the house to fall; but I do expect it will cease to be divided. It will become all one thing or all the other. Either the opponents of slavery will arrest the further spread of it, and place it where the public mind shall rest in the belief that it is in the course of ultimate extinction; or its advocates shall push it forward, till it shall become alike lawful in all the states, old as well as new, North as well as South.

It was clear to Lincoln and many others that the continental geography unified North and South. The historical barrier had been between East and West, not North and South, and the Atlantic Ocean and Ohio-Mississippi waterways only facilitated unity through north-south commerce. Tension over the moral division would never subside.

Senator Douglas pounced on the House Divided speech, leveraging it to portray Lincoln as a dangerous disunionist. Douglas's position was built on a pragmatic indifference as to whether slavery was right or wrong. It was a local issue only. He championed the idea that citizens of the territories ought to be permitted to decide for themselves—in true democratic fashion—whether their territory would be slave or free. He appealed to the principle, apart from moral consideration, that the union must be preserved, recognizing that any attempt to force a resolution of the moral question, no matter one way or the other, would lead to destruction of the union, and the need to steer well clear of that danger.

There were no intermissions in these debates. The orations were multi-issued, elaborate, and carefully reasoned. Much of the time was occupied with maneuvers on matters of local politics, attacks and rebuttals on personal integrity, and various representations and misrepresentations about who said what, where and when it was said, and what that meant. Each candidate scrutinized, questioned, and attempted to turn the other's past statements, positions, and legislative voting record into a political liability. In reading the text of the debates, much of this seems diversionary or of no consequence. Thus, matters involving principle did not occupy as much of the debates as one might have wished or expected. Yet, on the controversy that racked the nation in 1858, the positions of the candidates become clear as the chief and consequential difference between them. Douglas offered no high principles to guide. One choice was as good as another. One's view on slavery was a personal matter. In contrast, Lincoln reached back in history, snatched the high principles of liberty and equality under the rule of law out of the founders' revered wisdom, and stationed them up front, doing precisely what a nation in crisis needs.

The position of black persons in 1850's white America should be understood. Attitudes toward black equality among the white population, North as well as South, were almost universally negative. Without undertaking an analysis of the root of such attitudes, the circumstances of their presence in the Americas could be said to at least have contributed to the perception. Even when freed, after having been confined under an oppressive system and denied education, rising to higher levels of white cultural refinement was rare. Black persons were considered morally, socially, and intellectually inferior. It was a false perception, and irrationally persistent. To suggest, then, even the possibility of social and political equality between black and white was extremely unpopular, and to become associated with abolitionism was politically ruinous. Thus, it was necessary for Lincoln, in opposing Douglas's democratic moral indifference, to also maintain distance from abolition "extremism" as well. In this, he recognized no inconsistency between rights of life, liberty, and the pursuit of happiness guaranteed by the Declaration of Independence and an inferior social and political status.

The two orators also presented definite contrasts in both appearance and manner. Douglas at five feet four was combative and vigorous, impeccably appareled, and practiced in the art of public speaking. He was a "hurricane of passion" but also a model of verbal precision and rhetorical power, with finely structured sentences well strung together in clear and plausible oratory. In energy, mental agility, and fluency, Douglas was unmatched. Lincoln at six feet four was angular and gawky. Having a high-pitched, initially shrill voice, he was further described as seldom gesturing and seldom moving from position, though from time-to-time, he would move to the front of the speaker's platform with a particular gesture as if to hurl a point at the audience then walk slowly backward to again resume his speech from his original position. Yet in wit, dry humor, and relentless logic, Lincoln was supreme. The speaking styles of both men were learned and practiced according to their respective political party cultures. It was remarked by one observer that whereas Douglas's fury and magnetism would, in five minutes, make the greater impression, over an hour's time, Lincoln's more thoughtful and deliberate approach, together with the logical appeal of his arguments, would better commend him to his audience.[4]

The Illinois electorate maintained a Democratic Party majority in the Illinois legislature by a narrow margin in the November 1858 election. Douglas thereby held his Senate seat. But the debates were recorded by Chicago newspaper reporters skilled in shorthand and then printed in newspapers nationwide. The printed debates gave Lincoln national name recognition as someone who could survive and even thrive in confrontations with the all-powerful Douglas.

The 1860 election handed the presidency to Lincoln by the largest minority of votes in a four-way race between Douglas, who was nominated by the northern Democrats; Lincoln, the nominee of the Republicans; John Breckenridge of Kentucky, named by the southern Democrats; and John Bell of Tennessee, who ran as the candidate for the Constitutional Union Party, a hastily formed new party attempting to resurrect the old Whig platform. Then followed a sequence of events: South Carolina began a movement of southern states by seceding from the union on December 20, 1860; Jefferson Davis (1808–89) was inaugurated president of the confederate states on February 18, 1861; Lincoln was inaugurated president of the remaining states on March 4, 1861; and Fort Sumter was attacked by the Confederacy on April 12, 1861. Thus began the costliest war in US history. It is well to note that to his credit, Douglas threw his whole-hearted support behind Lincoln's goal of preserving the union before an untimely death on June 3, 1861.

In attempt to by-pass the intractable moral and political irresolution, the secession question—whether the states had a right to secede—has often been made to displace the slavery question and, to some degree, has overshadowed it. The Constitution said nothing about a right of states to secede from the union. Arguments, therefore, attempt to reach back before the Constitution to the revolutionary time period to justify either state sovereignty where the federal government is viewed as solely an agreement formed by the states, in support of the right to secede, or to defend the Constitution as a product of the sovereignty of the people collectively, and which only the people acting collectively could dissolve. The perpetuity of the union, predating the Constitution, was explicit in the Articles of Confederation and *Perpetual Union* (Article XIII), and which the Constitution only attempted to make "more perfect" as stated in its preamble. Notably, the Confederate Constitution contained no provision for a state to secede from it either.

The right of secession is now an academic question; there is no credible threat of disunion today. What is not an academic question is this: how could a principle as seemingly benign and as consistent with American political philosophy as popular sovereignty end up unleashing so much discord and strife? Was this a case of majority rule being proposed as the means to answer a question whose resolution could truly *not* be left to majority opinion? There is no need to discuss the moral nature of the slavery question other than to say that an aroused conscience may easily overwhelm any political or religious association. Political parties and religious denominations divided over this issue. Slavery has been the most contentious point of division ever faced by the nation. Though moral controversies are often discounted and even dismissed as irrelevant in the expediencies of politics, they are not so easily set aside in the minds of ordinary citizens. Lincoln did not need to argue beyond the Declaration of Independence in defense of the validity of the idea that all persons possess an intrinsic liberty that cannot be denied and that all should be equal under law. Merely to call attention to the Declaration was sufficient.

Appeal to the equality and liberty principles of the Declaration was ultimately effective and subsequently encoded in three constitutional amendments. The Thirteenth Amendment abolished slavery. The Fourteenth Amendment guaranteed the right of citizenship to former slaves and prevented any state from abridging "the privileges or immunities of citizens," from depriving "any person of life, liberty, or property without due process of law," and from denying "to any person within its jurisdiction the equal protection of the laws." The Fifteenth Amendment secured the right of citizens to vote irrespective of "race, color, or previous condition of servitude." The Fourteenth Amendment, however, was ratified under suspicious circumstances. The first attempt at ratification failed as all former Confederate states except Tennessee refused it, as did Maryland, Delaware, Kentucky, and California. In order to get the amendment passed, Congress organized new state governments in the former Confederacy under the Reconstruction Act of 1867. This act further required the new state legislatures to ratify the amendment as a condition for re-entering the union. In response to this manipulative tactic, Ohio and New Jersey rescinded their ratifications. The three-fourths Article V requirement for amendments was deemed satisfied when twenty-eight out of thirty-seven states had ratified it by July 1868, not counting Ohio and New Jersey.[5]

Section I of the Fourteenth Amendment seems consistent enough with the intent of the Declaration of Independence, the Constitution, and the Bill of Rights. The reluctance of the states is found in the fact that Section I is directed at them, not the federal government as is the case with the Bill of Rights. The intent of this section of the amendment was to prevent the states from reinstituting a form of slavery that would be slavery without calling it that. If that were all the amendment had been construed to mean, it might have achieved this end and then quietly passed out of notice. However, from the mid-twentieth century, the Supreme Court began to apply the amendment against the states on topics far beyond this original intent not only in selective application of the Bill of Rights to the states (the Supreme Court's "incorporation doctrine") but in other more recently construed rights unmentioned in the Bill of Rights or the Constitution's articles. By means of the Fourteenth Amendment, specifically its Equal Protection Clause, the Supreme Court has exerted enormous power over the states—power that was not to be found prior to the invention of new rights by the Court.

There is, nevertheless, another notable legacy emanating from the Lincoln-Douglas debates. While not disputing the fact that the Constitution intentionally contains no mention of any underlying political philosophy or metaphysical principle, the debates set in motion the chain of events that underscored its relation to another document which does. That the Constitution was thus amended means that it was and is inexorably bound to the philosophical grounds set forth in the Declaration of Independence. Liberty and the equal protections of law are propositions that come from somewhere, and that *somewhere* is a self-evidentness that has not gained greater presence than when backed by a creator.

Never before was this sort of liberty and equality at the individual level seen—not under the ancient civilizations of Greece and Rome, not under preceding ancient empires, not under Islamism, not under Hinduism, not under any of the Eastern civilizations, and not under the Western Hemisphere's primitive indigenous societies. No culture has been immune to the imposition of slavery and the rule of king above law. But in Western civilization, given the relentless logic of premises, a total moral reciprocity and equality of persons eventually prevailed. That logic is seen, among other developments, in the eventual removal of legalized slavery from Western civilization.

The removal occurred not once but twice, even while it remained profitable: first was when Western Europe during the medieval period shook off what it had inherited from the ancient world and second was when the African trade, introduced into the New World in the sixteenth century, was finally shut down in the nineteenth.[6] The equal moral standing of persons is an idea that can be traced to biblical roots even while the Bible appears to condone slavery.[7] For a nation whose central principles include equality under law and unalienable rights of liberty and the pursuit of happiness, the contradiction had to be resolved.

Federalist vs. Anti-Federalist

The Lincoln-Douglas debates, more than any other historical event, restored the central position of the 1776 Declaration of Independence in the consciousness of America. That is why they were presented first. Now we turn to the central place of the 1787 Constitution that is best understood and appreciated by observing the debates over its ratification.

After more than three months of proposals and counter proposals, contention, and compromise, the Constitutional Convention in Philadelphia finally completed their work on September 17, 1787. What they had in hand, though, was only a proposed constitution. As stated in the last article, Article VII, the ratifying conventions of at least nine states had to approve it. In this, the Constitution that today is taken for granted came close to becoming a historical relic.

The extent of opposition to the Constitution and the closeness of the ratification votes in some of the larger and more influential state conventions are not as generally known as they perhaps ought to be. Some of the state conventions nearly rejected it, and only through conditions being attached to their resolutions was a positive outcome attained. In Massachusetts, the ratification vote was 187 yeas to 168 nays with a call for numerous substantial amendments. In Virginia, the count was 89 to 79 with a call for numerous substantial amendments. In New York, the vote was 30 to 27 with, again, a call for numerous substantial amendments. In North Carolina, the first ratifying convention failed to ratify by 83 to 184, and a second was called the following year. Rhode Island had neglected to send delegates to the Philadelphia Convention and initially rejected ratification by popular vote, not even troubling to debate the matter in open convention. They eventually called a convention in 1790, voting 34 to 32 to ratify. Even within the Constitutional Convention itself, there had been disappointment and doubt. Of the 55 delegates sent to Philadelphia, 16 did not sign the finished document.

No sooner had the proposed constitution been made public, opposition made itself known. Some of the most well-known names of the Revolution—Patrick Henry, George Mason, and Richard Henry Lee of Virginia—argued against ratification. Elbridge Gerry, Samuel Adams, and John Hancock of Massachusetts also opposed it, though the latter two helped to work out a compromise by which ratification in their state was enabled. Two of the three delegates to the 1787 Philadelphia Constitutional Convention from New York, Robert Yates and John Lansing, had left the convention early in protest. Melancton Smith and Governor George Clinton stirred up opposition to ratification in New York State. The most vigorous opposition to ratification, in fact, arose in New York State, provoking Alexander Hamilton, the only remaining delegate and signer of the Constitution from New York, to organize counter arguments. Enlisting the aid of James Madison and John Jay, he began a series of newspaper articles in defense of the proposed constitution during the ratification proceedings of the individual states during 1787–88. These articles were collected and came to be called The Federalist Papers (of which there are 85). Robert Yates, James Winthrop, Samuel Bryan, John Francis Mercer, and others, including some anonymous, unknown authors, wrote a similar series of articles and letters arguing against ratification. These became known as the Anti-Federalist papers.

In order to better understand the debate over ratification, it is necessary to back up to the situation prior to the Philadelphia convention. The Articles of Confederation and Perpetual Union comprised the first national constitution. They established a single congress only; there was no judiciary or executive branch. The

Articles of Confederation authorized the congress to deal only with foreign policy and defense, disputes between states, interstate and foreign commerce, and matters pertaining to territories. Each state retained its internal sovereignty and independence. The Articles were approved by Congress on November 15, 1777, and ratified by the last state, Maryland, on March 1, 1781. They remained in force until March 4, 1789 when the present constitution replaced them.

Although the Articles of Confederation served to bring the thirteen states into concerted action in administering the Revolutionary War, they were viewed by many as inadequate to deal with numerous problems confronting the confederation that had arisen during and after the war. Congress under the articles lacked authority over the states to force them to fulfill treaty obligations with respect to the property of those who had remained loyal to the British government and which property had been confiscated during the revolution. This resulted in reciprocal lapses of England to honor its treaty obligations. There was a failure to secure borders with Spain and to secure access to the Mississippi River. There was a failure to protect American shipping on the high seas. There was a failure to pay war debts, and as a consequence, the nation had no credit standing. Congress had no enforcement authority over the states and thus none over individual citizens who were only accountable to state authority. There was no mechanism to force states to fulfill their revenue obligations to Congress. In effect, the national government was dependent on "donations" from the states. Treaties had to be ratified by the individual states. Congress had no authority to enforce its legislation. The states had to do it. All effective political power remained with the states. Laws passed by Congress were practically only recommendations to the states. The states themselves, conscious of their individual independence, engaged in petty squabbles over tariffs against other states.

Therefore, on February 21, 1787, Congress endorsed a proposal for a convention to propose amendments to the Articles. But that convention, in closed secret meeting, produced instead a brand new constitution, a complete and unprecedented departure from the Articles, appealing not to Congress who authorized it, nor to the state governments, but to special state ratifying conventions whose delegates were to be elected by citizens of each state. That was not what Congress had intended, and there is perhaps little wonder as to why opposition rose up at once.

Federalist and Anti-Federalist Positioning

The Anti-Federalists spoke as conservatives opposing ratification. Stressing the need for citizen participation, they saw the balance of power weighted toward state governments as the ideal. They noted the absence of any provision for the states to "check" the national government in the proposed constitution. The strong national government being advocated by the Federalists under the proposed constitution seemed too much like the very thing from which the states had fought the Revolution to gain release. On the basis of this concern, notes professor Thomas L. Pangle, the Anti-Federalists began an appeal to certain distinctive aspects of the ancient Greek and Roman republican governments: their ideals of direct citizen participation in legislation and decision-making, public virtue, and a religiously or ideologically homogeneous citizenry.[8]

Ancient republican style governments were predicated on direct participation of citizens. Governments modeled on this classical republican ideal had, therefore, to be small enough in geography and population to facilitate that participation. If the individual states, especially the larger ones, were hardly qualified in that respect, certainly not all of them together. Public virtue was the concern of the average citizen for the common good, which was made both relevant and desirable by the citizen's participation. Religious or ideological homogeneity was necessary to avoid excessive internal conflict and strife. The Anti-Federalists were committed to religious liberty, yet they hedged that by saying that religious liberty should be restricted to Protestant forms of Christianity. They noted the lack of any provision in the proposed constitution for government support of education that would instill civic virtue and the lack of any acknowledgment of the authority of God. Some of them were put off by the constitution's prohibition of any religious test for office in Article VI. How would civic virtue be maintained, they argued, without any deference to religion under the proposed constitution? On these points, they concluded that the proposed constitution was an unprecedented and unjustified departure from the traditional republican model.[9]

In the aspect of citizen participation, it is true that homogeneity and smallness were not what either the Anti-Federalists or the Federalists expected to be the future of America. In considering the vastness and diversity of the United States, even in 1787–88, some departure from the ancient republican ideal was necessary at the national level as both sides envisioned the nation's future as far larger in population, geographic extent, and commercial diversity than historical republican formulas could ever accommodate. This is why the Anti-Federalists, being committed to traditional republican liberty, were reluctant to release more power from the states to a national government. The Anti-Federalist's conservative focus on the ideals of citizen participation and a religiously motivated civic virtue was necessary, they contended, to counter aristocratic ambition and the corrupting tendencies of politics.[10]

To this position, the Federalists advanced no counter argument but turned the debate onto a whole new front: national security, foreign policy, and the danger of a disintegrating union. The Federalists argued that the seriousness of foreign threats could not be overestimated and that a strong central government was necessary to thwart them. They stressed the need to enforce adherence of both states and citizens to international law, custom, and treaty obligations to avoid provoking foreign powers. They stressed the need to deter foreign powers from envious dispositions, from sowing disunity, and from taking advantage of the weaknesses of a loose confederacy to encroach on national independence. The states, they observed, inevitably wrangle against each other and, thereby, produce tempting opportunities for foreign intrigue and meddling.

In principle and in history, the Federalists further argued, the inherent frailty of confederacies renders them inadequate to secure against foreign threats and no number of amendments to the Articles of Confederation could fix that. They emphasized the need for a standing national army and navy as a deterrent, even in peacetime, to this end. They believed that unlimited military power was necessary to thwart foreign threats and, therefore, a need for unlimited taxation power to achieve that so as not to have to appeal to state governments to gain necessary revenue. The Federalists thus insisted that there be no (and the Constitution contains no provision for any) limitation on military and taxation power of the national government.[11]

To this, the Anti-Federalists retorted that governments universally find a use for whatever spending and taxation powers are given to them.[12] And yes, Alexander Hamilton (1755–1804) agreed, maintaining this as reason for the national taxation power in Federalist 30:

> I believe it may be regarded as a position warranted by the history of mankind that, in the usual progress of things, the necessities of a nation, in every stage of its existence, will be found at least equal to its resources.

What realistic alternative proposal, asked the Federalists, did the Anti-Federalists have for squaring up to external dangers?

Despite these seemingly intractable differences, there was common ground: a commitment to the republican form of government.[13] The Federalists were as committed to the republican cause as the Anti-Federalists. Madison stated in Federalist 39:

> The first question that offers itself is whether the general form and aspect of the government be strictly republican. It is evident that no other form would be reconcilable with the genius of the people of America, with the fundamental principles of the revolution, or with that honorable determination which animates every votary of freedom to rest all our political experiments on the capacity of mankind for self-government. If the plan of the convention [referring to the 1787 Philadelphia Convention's proposed constitution], therefore, be found

to depart from the republican character, its advocates must abandon it as no longer defensible.

Both Federalists and Anti-Federalists regarded the traditional virtuous image of classical republican governments highly, and many of them wrote under pen names after Roman statesmen, such as Cato, Brutus, Centinel, and Publius. Hamilton, James Madison (1751–1836), and John Jay (1745–1829) all wrote under the pen name Publius. But Hamilton, in Federalist 9, argued that the nation would be ill-advised to follow the classical models of ancient Greece and Rome, which had proven to be so unstable in their vulnerability to majority whim and a tendency to swing between tyranny and anarchy. The Federalists saw a need for substantial deviation from the classical republican ideal, and they readily acknowledged the proposed constitution's departure from that. Through more recent innovations in the science of politics, better republican formulas were now available. The proposed constitution, Hamilton contended in Federalist 9, would avoid the weaknesses that had always haunted republican governments in the past, weaknesses that made them too vulnerable to either tyrannical majorities or despots that gain the trust of a majority.

But how did the Federalists propose to check the national government from becoming despotic under the proposed constitution? How did they intend to prevent the swallowing up of the state governments, given that the state governments would become subordinate and given the national government's unlimited taxation power? And what about the proposed constitution would thwart the "artful misrepresentations of interested men," as Madison so aptly described in Federalist 63 that chief threat to liberty from taking over government? It was bad enough that some persons should trample the rights of others, but what was to prevent the national government, the chief responsibility of which should be to uphold the rights of citizens and attend to the administration of justice, from doing just that? Professor Pangle concludes that the Federalists failed to offer satisfying answers to these points in so far as the state governments would be involved. Though Madison repeatedly advanced the argument that the states choose their senators and the president via the electoral process, the Anti-Federalists remained unpersuaded that these provisions gave effective checking power to the states.[14]

On this unresolved dilemma, the proper vision of a republic, the future of the United States hung in the balance. Were there any means to find middle ground between the state sovereignty preferred by the Anti-Federalists where the states were sufficiently strong and independent to be able to resist national encroachments into their affairs and thus a fragile union versus the Federalists' proposed constitution where the states were gathered under the domain of a strong central government and little able to withstand its power though secure against foreign intrusion?

The Constitution's Republican Design

Madison and Hamilton acknowledged that vast authority was being granted to the national government in the proposed constitution. What made this safe to do, they wrote, was the separation of powers and the system of checks and balances within the government itself. While Anti-Federalists argued that the checks and balances should be between state and national governments, Madison and Hamilton called attention to the balancing and regulation of competing interests within the national government itself. The proposed constitution, they explained, contained an internal system of checks and balances between legislative, executive, and judicial powers. Each branch was empowered with certain limited means to regulate the actions of the other two toward the end that a majority interest, if overtaking one branch, could not easily coalesce and act in unison within the whole. The states and citizens were excluded from direct involvement in this system.

The key, then, to keeping the powerful national government of the proposed constitution in check was to be found in keeping majority interests within the national government in check. In Federalist 10, Madison named the tendency of majority interests to hijack democratic governments to serve their own purposes at the expense of everyone else as the *violence of faction*. It is "this dangerous vice" that has been the cause of the "instability, injustice, and confusion introduced into the public councils," he wrote, and "under which popular governments have everywhere perished."

More than anything else, observed Madison, the problem of factions (what today would be called special interest groups) has been, throughout history, the central problem of free government. In the same paper, Madison defined a faction as

> A number of citizens, whether amounting to a majority or minority of the whole, who are united and actuated by some common impulse of passion, or of interest, adverse to the rights of other citizens, or to the permanent and aggregate interests of the community.

Observing that the violence of faction was active even in the state governments at the time, he continued,

> The public good is disregarded in the conflicts of rival parties, and measures are too often decided, not according to the rules of justice and the rights of the minority party, but by the superior force of an interested and overbearing majority… [The] prevailing and increasing distrust of public engagements and alarm for private rights which are echoed from one end of the continent to the other must be chiefly, if not wholly, effects of the unsteadiness and injustice with which a factious spirit has tainted our public administration.

Continuing in Federalist 10, Madison further expounded on the purpose at hand:

> To secure the public good and private rights against the danger of such [majority] factions, and at the same time to preserve the spirit and the form of popular government, is then the great object to which our inquiries are directed.

Legislatures alone could not be depended upon to mediate the problem of faction because the majority becomes judge of its own cause. A more elaborate scheme was necessary.

Beginning to build the case for the proposed constitution, Madison explained that there are two approaches to curing the mischiefs of faction: (1) removing its causes and (2) controlling its effects. The two means of removing its causes—despotism, the removal of liberty to even express opinions, or somehow producing the same opinions, passions, and interests—are worse than faction itself. Either of these forced removals of faction runs counter to human nature and liberty. In reference to the first means, the suppression of liberty is exactly opposite to what is sought in the first place. In reference to the second means, while the Anti-Federalists, following the classical republican model, sought means to suppress the emergence of factions by promoting virtue and homogeneity of opinion among the citizens, Madison summarily dismissed such possibility. It would be foolish, he contended, to think that naturally occurring division and animosity could be contained.

> So strong is this propensity of mankind to fall into mutual animosities, that where no substantial occasion presents itself, the most frivolous and fanciful distinctions have been sufficient to kindle their unfriendly passions and excite their most violent conflicts.

Madison instead turned to controlling the effects of faction. The solution must not be to eliminate factions but rather to prevent majority factions from being able to exert their will and to do that while yet preserving the liberty of factions to have a will.

One of two developments, wrote Madison in reference to the controlling of effects, must be produced to thwart the power of majority factions: either prevent the same passion or interest present in a majority from coalescing and collaborating in the first place, or given a majority faction already in existence, render it unable to effect schemes of oppression. The tyranny of the majority must be prevented. He went on to say that each of these first requires a representative form of government that puts the decision-making authority of the people at a distance. The filtering of popular opinion through representatives would be expected to "refine and enlarge the public views." When somewhat detached from popular will by a medium of representation, a forum of deliberation—deliberation which direct participation of the people in decision-making could never accommodate—would be more likely to act on the aggregate interests rather than factional interests. Additionally, and most critically, a diverse and geographically extensive population characterized as a complex of numerous competing interests and passions was to be the key—a faction ridden populace that, by geographic expanse and regional diversity, would be unable to achieve the self-awareness that would bring it into being as a single majority faction. In contrast to the Anti-Federalist desire to suppress the emergence of factions, Madison contended that the problem of factions would itself actually become the solution. Faction would combat faction.

Within the national government itself, then, a system of internally conflicting interactions between house, senate, executive, and judiciary would neutralize the power of majority factions. In the proposed constitution, each branch would be equipped with limited measures of authority over the others so as to check their power. This is the system of checks and balances. Both houses of congress must pass any legislation. The president can veto legislation. Congress can override a veto by a two-thirds majority of both houses. While the president is commander-in-chief of the armed forces, Congress sets the armed forces' budget and decides when to go to war. The Supreme Court can void legislation in cases brought before it, but the legislature can restrict the appellate jurisdiction of the Court. The Senate must consent to the president's selection of Supreme Court Justices and any treaties negotiated.

Here, it is also worth noting that house, senate, and executive correlate generally to the standard governmental forms of democracy, aristocracy, and monarchy respectively. The nature of the House and Senate would offset each other. The democratic-oriented House would represent closely the will of the people, being popularly elected and having short two-year terms. The more aristocratic Senate, the representative vehicle of the states, would possess greater stability with its staggered six-year terms. The decisive character of a single monarchical executive would offset the deliberative quality of the legislature. The merging of democracy, aristocracy, and monarchy into a single composite interlocking system would mitigate the historically well-known tyrannical dangers of any one such system by itself.

The Federalist vision was that each branch would be in competition against the others to dominate the government. "Ambition must be made to counteract ambition. The interest of the man must be connected with the constitutional rights of the place" (*place* referring to the particular branch) wrote Madison in Federalist 51. Thus, an ambitious branch, attempting to gain the upper hand, would be checked by the similar ambitions of the others. No branch on its own would be able to run the government. If anything was to be done, all three branches would need to reach agreement. Such agreement would require alignment of opinion among citizens over time. The influence of majority factions emerging among the people during brief periods would be filtered out by the staggered terms of office in the system of elections for house, senate, and executive. Continuing discord of opinion would prevent government action by the checks and balances between house, senate, executive, and judicial. Only following a sustained prevalence of opinion among the citizens could the branches of government align and take concerted action. The expectation was that government would be deadlocked on any matter on which there was no general agreement over time among the people. However, the expectation of thwarting majority factions by numerous competing factions is now often nullified by consolidation of interest groups into political parties. The Constitution's defenses against majority faction tend to be confounded at those times when House, Senate, and the president are aligned to one or the other of the two parties. This is a development that seems not to have been anticipated at the time of the debate.

In answer to the Anti-Federalist concern for virtue, Madison and Hamilton argued that a certain level of virtue would be produced by the distancing of representatives from the populace. The Federalists did not discount the need for virtue but envisioned that as being present among the representatives. Whereas the Anti-Federalists were concerned about corruption of virtue among the representatives, the Federalists were concerned about oppressive tendencies of majority faction arising within the populace. The Federalists contended that the best means to promote civic virtue is by having a strong central government that would motivate and inspire in the most talented and virtuous citizens a desire for public service. Thus, the Anti-Federalist vision depended on virtue within the populace while the Federalist vision depended on virtue in the representatives. Was either view realistic? And what would secure civic virtue in anyone in the first place? Was there any means to establish this precondition that both sides viewed as a necessary component of civil liberty while, at the same time, guaranteeing religious liberty?

We will return to this question in the next chapter. For now, it is obvious that the appeal of the Federalist vision prevailed; the proposed constitution was formally ratified on June 21, 1788, when the ninth state, New Hampshire, approved it by a vote of 57 to 47. The Federalist plan prevailed again in the 1861–65 War Between the States when state sovereignty gave way to the preservation of the union.

The Bill of Rights

Of the many and various questions over specific provisions in the Constitution, certain heavily debated particulars between Federalists and Anti-Federalists stand out. Should representatives in the House be elected to one-or two-year terms? What was the optimal number of representatives in the House and, thereby, the number of constituents per representative? What was to be the degree of overlap of powers between House, Senate, executive (presidency), and judicial? Was it best to have a single executive presidency or an executive council?

But the one theme that the Anti-Federalists sounded over and over was a bill of rights. A bill of rights was also the one concession eventually granted to the Anti-Federalists—a bill of rights in the form of a series of amendments. The Federalists argued against such an incursion into the proposed constitution on the ground that the design of the constitution itself was sufficient to guarantee individual rights. The powers of the national government spelled out in Article 1, Section 8, were few and defined. Powers not specifically delegated to the national government by the constitution were automatically retained by the states or the people. And since it would be impossible to list all rights that could ever be challenged by the government, any rights that did not end up on the list might become fair game for infringement later on.

Many of the states, though, had bills of rights in their constitutions. The Federalists were eventually persuaded to accept a bill of rights as a practical necessity for winning over at least some Anti-Federalists. A bill of rights consisting of ten amendments was attached to the Constitution by the first congress and ratified by the states in 1791. The bill was not exactly what the Anti-Federalists had desired—it did not restore any of the powers taken away from the states and given to the federal government; it did not remove a standing army in peacetime; it did not specify limitations on central government authority to tax and regulate the economy; and it did not identify the rights of states. Nevertheless, this contribution of the Anti-Federalists to the Constitution has proven its value. One has only to consider where individual rights and liberties might be today without some of these amendments.

The Bill of Rights itemizes what the national government cannot do against its citizens and the policies it is obligated to observe in its administration of justice in the first eight amendments. Know for certain that the Bill of Rights does no such thing as granting these rights. Rather, it merely puts restrictions on government to not interfere with, or else to respect, *already existing* rights. The itemization includes the right to determine and practice one's religious beliefs, the right to public speech, to form associations, to own and carry firearms, to control the use of one's property, to be secure against unwarranted searches or seizures, and certain rights of anyone accused of a crime. The list is not exhaustive; the last two entries cover rights not otherwise specified, that is, whatever other pre-existing rights might ever be described.

The Ninth Amendment states,

> The enumeration in the Constitution of certain rights shall not be construed to deny or disparage others retained by the people.

The Tenth Amendment states,

> Powers not delegated to the United States by the Constitution, nor prohibited by it to the states, are reserved to the states, respectively, or to the people.

The Ninth and Tenth amendments do not mean that any non-enumerated right or non-delegated power may be claimed by anyone or by any state. The question as to which rights not enumerated and which powers not delegated are legitimate to be held by the states or the people and which are not was left open. Should any such right or power be contested, it would have to be "reserved to" or "retained by" the states or the people by becoming law through the constitutional amendment process or by legislation. That is all that may be said from a constitutional point of view.

Concluding Remarks

The most notable advantage of the Federalists' position is that they had a well-defined and thought-through solution: the proposed constitution. The Anti-Federalists never came up with a coherent alternative plan to deal with the deficiencies of the Articles of Confederation. Yet in their critique of the proposed constitution, they raised awareness of tendencies and dangers that remain relevant today:

1. The tendency toward centralization of power and expansion of the scope and size of bureaucracies, particularly when given unlimited taxation power, a power now augmented by the Federal Reserve Bank's ability to expand (or inflate) the currency supply, thus instituting a hidden taxation through controlled devaluation.

2. The danger of corruption in the absence of a system for maintaining a basis of civic virtue, a basis that may now be diminishing from whatever ambient religious basis was present in earlier times.
3. The tendency toward aristocratic elitism in the absence of direct citizen participation, an elitism that presumes to know what is best for the people and that is now augmented by the presumption of scientific expertise and the legal proceduralism characteristic of bureaucracies against which the average citizen is pretty helpless.

Today also, the role of the states in containing the tendency of the national government to outgrow its constitutional box is effectively thwarted by the national government's bribing of the states into partnering in its extra-constitutional initiatives.

The Federalists and Anti-Federalists were both reluctant to place great trust anywhere. The Federalists veered against placing too much in the people, while the Anti-Federalists against too much in the representatives and national government. Whichever side one might be inclined to favor, it is true that the placement of trust, though necessary to place somewhere, is a serious problem. The Constitution itself perhaps ought to be considered a worthy repository of trust, but that seems less and less likely. With all the present day expectations and demands that the national government intervene to fix many problems, there seems little chance that anything like the Constitution could be agreed upon if the ratification debates were held today. We often see it being thrust aside in a rush to plunder the public treasury under a pretense of doing good. Should more and more of the wealth of the nation continue to get thus routed through its capitol, the capitol would become a cancerous growth that could eventually kill the patient.

Federalist vs. Anti-Federalist II: Judicial Review

A component of the Federalist–Anti-Federalist debate that should not be overlooked was the dispute over judicial review. Judicial review refers to the authority of the judicial branch, specifically the Supreme Court, to declare legislation unconstitutional and thus null and void. In recent decades especially, this authority has become an instrument of unchecked and unbalanced power and explains why Senate confirmation of Supreme Court nominees is often so contentious. It is necessary, then, to follow the debate over this topic also as the proposed constitution was set before the state ratifying conventions.

Who really has the final say as to the constitutionality of anything the government might legislate? Should the Supreme Court be the final or even exclusive determiner of constitutionality? If senators, congressmen, judges, and all other public officials, federal as well as state, are all required by Article VI to support the Constitution, what is their role in judging the constitutionality of any action? Article VI states, "The Senators and Representatives before mentioned, and the Members of the several State Legislatures, and all executive and judicial Officers, both of the United States and of the several States, shall be bound by Oath or Affirmation to support this Constitution." Unless these office holders understand the meaning of the Constitution, their affirmation to support it would seem to be pointless; it should not require special legal expertise to know whether something is acceptable under the Constitution. The president is required under Article II, Section I to "preserve, protect, and defend the Constitution." Likewise, the president would not be able to fulfill this obligation unless the meaning of the Constitution is clear to the president.

Judicial review is not explicitly mentioned in the Constitution. But it is commonly taken for granted that the Supreme Court is the final determiner of constitutionality. Where did that idea come from and why was it disputed? The debate over judicial review took place chiefly between Alexander Hamilton (1755–1804) writing as Publius and Anti-Federalist Brutus whom historians suspect may have been Robert Yates (1738–1801) of New York.

Article III, Section 2 of the Constitution states, "The judicial Power shall extend to all Cases, in Law and Equity, arising under this Constitution." Anti-Federalist Brutus began in Letter XI to contend that "equity" in this context, and as taught by authorities such as English Jurist William Blackstone (1723–80), means judging according to the spirit of the law, even outside of or in contradiction to the letter of the law, or to judge according to implicit intentions of the legislature. The appearance of this term, Brutus continued in Letter XV, puts the Supreme Court above the legislature:

> In the exercise of this power they [the judiciary] will not be subordinate to but above the legislature. . . The legislature can only exercise such powers as are given them by the constitution; they cannot assume any of the rights annexed to the judicial, for this plain reason, that the same authority which vested the legislature with their powers, vested the judicial with theirs... The supreme court then have a right, independent of the legislature, to give a construction to the constitution and every part of it, and there is no power provided in this system to correct their construction or do it away. If, therefore, the legislature pass any laws, inconsistent with the sense the judges put upon the constitution, they will declare it void, and therefore in this respect their power is superior to that of the legislature.

Pointing out that such judicial power had never been heard of in the entire history of republican liberty, including that of the thirteen colonies, Brutus remarked on the implications of the proposed supreme court's superiority:

> I question whether the world ever saw, in any period of it, a court of justice invested with such immense powers and yet placed in a situation so little responsible... The judges under this constitution will controul the legislature, for the supreme court are authorised in the last resort, to

determine what is the extent of the powers of the Congress, they are to give the constitution an explanation, and there is no power above them to set aside their judgment... They are independent of the people, of the legislature, and of every power under heaven. Men placed in this situation will generally soon feel themselves independent of heaven itself.

In these sentences, the absence of any recourse to the proposed supreme court's decisions declaring acts of the legislature unconstitutional and void under the proposed constitution was abundantly clarified.

Other Anti-Federalists, recognizing that courts possess distinct moral and legal authority and influence, seconded the concern.[15] The proposed supreme court, they observed, with its unelected members, lifetime tenure, whose decisions are debated in secret and who exercise the final appeal over legislation, will be unaccountable to the people. In this, the court will be able to nullify even constitutional legislation and to subordinate the people's own elected representatives.[16] Thus, the Anti-Federalist writing as The Federal Farmer (possibly Richard Henry Lee) in his own Letter XV wrote:

> We may fairly conclude, we are more in danger of sowing the seeds of arbitrary government in this department than in any other.

Publius, from Federalist 78 onward, began an extensive counterargument defending the proposed judicial branch. Hamilton writing here first denied that judicial review causes the judiciary to be superior to the legislature. The judicial, he wrote, is the "least dangerous" branch having no power over the purse or the sword, and thus it "can take no active resolution whatever." While Hamilton affirmed the Supreme Court's power of judicial review, he did not share Brutus's view on the meaning of the term *equity* in Article III, Section 2.

In defense of the judicial power, explains professor Pangle, Hamilton appealed not to wording in the proposed constitution but rather to two general principles: (1) that judicial review is intrinsic to the nature of constitutions that express the will of the people and (2) that it is the proper and even intrinsic province of the courts rather than the legislature to interpret the laws including the supreme and fundamental law, the Constitution.[17] Hamilton argued that the Supreme Court, in being able to declare legislation unconstitutional rather than over-ruling the people's will, would be expressing the ultimate will of the people. This would be achieved by upholding the constitutional limits of the legislature—that is, as he wrote, "to keep the later within the limits of their authority," and by not allowing the people's constitution to be set aside even by the people's elected representatives. Hamilton asserted that judicial review is implicit in the idea of an overruling constitution, established and ordained by the sovereignty of the people and with which no law can stand in opposition. It is justified on the basis that there must be a check on the possibility that the legislative power could exceed the limits of its own constitutional authority.

Here was Hamilton's first point in defense of judicial review, arguing that the people's direction for government provided in their constitution is best served when the people's elected representatives are constrained by the courts against transgressions of their constitution. The judiciary may, therefore, need to stand against the legislature and, perhaps, even the people themselves if temporarily swept up in some temptation to subvert their own constitution. In this, they would be upholding the people's fundamental law. To his second point, Hamilton went on to argue that the judicial function is uniquely qualified to interpret the law, including the Constitution itself, more so than the legislature. The reason he provided was his expectation that the judges would be of superior intellect and moral judgment and would possess greater legal expertise and experience as compared to elected representatives. He saw reasonable grounds for placing the country's trust in such selected superior individuals.

So here, we have the Federalist claim that it is better to trust the judiciary with final authority on the constitutionality of laws passed by the legislature over against the Anti-Federalist apprehension of the danger of assigning this power to a very few unelected, life-tenured, and largely unaccountable Supreme Court justices. As in the debate over state versus national predominance, it does not appear that there was any possibility of a balanced resolution to the concerns expressed by the two opposing camps.

The Federalists prevailed, of course, and the question remains: Who checks the Supreme Court if it should go awry? It has not always been merely an academic question. In the mid-twentieth century, the Supreme Court began to apply a means to strike down state laws bearing on matters of individual liberty—Section 1 of the Fourteenth Amendment. The Fourteenth Amendment was, as previously noted, ratified in 1868 under irregular circumstances. Southern state ratification of the Thirteenth Amendment was accepted by Congress, whereas rejection of the Fourteenth by the very same states was invalidated by Congress. The Fourteenth Amendment has introduced the possibility of review and oversight of state laws by federal courts in matters far beyond what it was intended to achieve at the time it was ratified. The use of Section 1 of the amendment to require states to recognize selected provisions of the Bill of Rights is certainly within the bounds of the Supreme Court's authority under the Fourteenth Amendment, whatever the amendment's history. Prior to that, the Bill of Rights restrained the federal government only. But the Supreme Court, on its own authority, the very danger expressed by the Anti-Federalists, has also required the states to recognize individual rights not found in the Constitution. In this, the Supreme Court has engaged in extra-constitutional law-making activity, an example of which is found in the following section.

Congress has the constitutional authority to limit the appellate jurisdiction of the Supreme Court under Article III, Section 2 but has always been reluctant to use that check. On this matter, then, of judicial review, an admonition of the third president of the United States, Thomas Jefferson (1743–1826) is well to note:

> On every question of construction, [we should] carry ourselves back to the time when the Constitution was adopted, recollect the spirit manifested in the debates, and instead of trying what meaning may be squeezed out of the

text, or invented against it, conform to the probable one in which it was passed. Our peculiar security is in possession of a written constitution. Let us not make it a blank paper by construction.[18]

To this, President Lincoln in his first inaugural address added,

> I do not forget the position assumed by some, that constitutional questions are to be decided by the Supreme Court; nor do I deny that such decisions must be binding in any case, upon the parties to a suit, as to the object of that suit, while they are also entitled to very high respect and consideration, in all parallel cases, by all departments of the government... At the same time, the candid citizen must confess that if the policy of the government, upon vital questions, affecting the whole people, is to be irrevocably fixed by decisions of the Supreme Court, the instant they are made, in ordinary litigation between parties, in personal actions, the people will have ceased to be their own rulers.

A Moral Controversy Before the Court

On occasion, questions of a moral and controversial nature for which there is little, if any, guidance found in the Constitution end up before the Supreme Court. Of all the controversial cases ever heard by the Supreme Court, the 1973 case of *Roe v. Wade* certainly ranks at or near the top in controversy. Here, the Supreme Court considered the existence of an individual right of privacy and a right to terminate a pregnancy in decisions to seek an abortion and for access to abortions. These rights were offset by a state's interest (the state of Texas in the particular case) in protecting the health of women that could be endangered by the "procedure" and the state's interest in preserving human life before birth. The Court ruled that a state may regulate the abortion procedure only as these interests reach a "compelling" point at various stages in pregnancy, with that point being defined by the Court as subsequent to the first trimester as regards the health of the mother and subsequent to the "viability" stage—the stage at which an unborn baby is likely to survive outside the womb—as regards the preservation of life. Restrictions without regard to the stage of pregnancy were declared unconstitutional:

> The Texas authorities will doubtless fully recognize the Court's ruling that the Texas criminal abortion statutes are unconstitutional.

It does not take much of a studied read through the Constitution to realize that there is nothing in it that would guide the weighing of a right to privacy, a right to terminate a pregnancy, and stages of pregnancy and viability against a state's interests over health and life. The Court obviously had to steer its way through the tangle of opinions on the abortion matter using its own sense of justice. We may consider here some further excerpts from the Court's opinion as an example of its exercise of the sense of its responsibilities under the Fourteenth Amendment.

The Court summarized its majority opinion as follows:

> State criminal abortion laws, like those involved here, that except from criminality only a life-saving procedure on the mother's behalf without regard to the stage of her pregnancy and other interests involved violate the Due Process Clause of the Fourteenth Amendment, which protects against state action the right to privacy, including a woman's qualified right to terminate her pregnancy. Though the state cannot override that right, it has legitimate interests in protecting both the pregnant woman's health and the potentiality of human life, each of which interests grows and reaches a 'compelling' point at various stages of the woman's approach to term.

The Court was careful to balance various considerations:

> This holding, we feel, is consistent with the relative weights of the respective interests involved, with the lessons and examples of medical and legal history, with the lenity of the common law, and with the demands of the profound problems of the present day.

But any moral sensibilities are written off early in the opinion:

> We forthwith acknowledge our awareness of the sensitive and emotional nature of the abortion controversy, of the vigorous opposing views, even among physicians, and of the deep and seemingly absolute convictions that the subject inspires. One's philosophy, one's experiences, one's exposure to the raw edges of human existence, one's religious training, one's attitude toward life and family and their values, and the moral standards one establishes and seeks to observe, are all likely to influence and to color one's thinking and conclusions about abortion.

It is clear that the Court was alert to the possibility of such influences and colorations and intended to not be so influenced and colored.

The opinion continues to expound on the Court's balancing challenges:

> In addition, population growth, pollution, poverty, and racial overtones tend to complicate and not to simplify the problem.

In all this, the Court did not overlook its obligation to rule with respect to the Constitution:

> Our task, of course, is to resolve the issue by constitutional measurement, free of emotion and of predilection.

But it appears that the Court implicitly recognized the lack of any constitutional criterion because the opinion begins to review the history of abortion for insight as if casting about for something upon which to hang a decision. It considers ancient historical views regarding the "procedure," the Hippocratic Oath, Common Law, English Statutory Law, pre-existing American Law on the subject, the views of the American Medical Association, the American Public Health Association, and the American Bar Association.

The question of whether privacy is a right protected by the Constitution was considered. The Court's opinion affirms a view that either the Ninth or the Fourteenth Amendment is sufficient to assert such a right, but that such a right cannot be absolute. On this basis, the opinion insists that a state must balance its interests in protecting health and life against the right to privacy. The opinion dismisses the view that life begins at conception as not having the necessary historical qualification or legal precedence; no meaning of the term *person* as it appears in the Fourteenth Amendment is found in the historical or legal record that would supply a precedent for such a definition as might include an unborn child. So in the general confusion and multiplicity of views on exactly when life begins, the opinion abandons further consideration of that—*We need not resolve the difficult question of when life begins*—and instead settles on the idea of viability.

A number of questions surface: Can the Supreme Court, or any court, unilaterally assert a right unmentioned in the Constitution such as a right to privacy? Is it not rather the people that collectively through their legislatures, in view of the Ninth Amendment, that must decide whether to retain an unmentioned right? Why should the Court not be "colored" by values and morals if they are going to take up a topic loaded with them and one for which the Constitution has nothing to say? Why was there no recognition of the bare facts that the embryo is alive, that it is human, and that the "procedure" destroys it? In all its technical virtuosity, something is missing from the Court's opinion. The Court ruled that to a certain point, a right of privacy should prevail over that of life. But the only historical precedents to be found anywhere, such as the Ten Commandments or the Declaration of Independence, station the right to life as inviolable, not a right to privacy.

The dissenting opinion of chief justice William Rehnquist, while raising important legal-technical inconsistencies also bypasses moral aspects: (1) the question about the status of plaintiff's pregnancy at time of suit raised a question as to the hypothetical nature of the case; (2a) the "due process of law" phrase of the Fourteenth Amendment would seem to have been satisfied by the state; (2b) the conscious weighing of various factors in the opinion of the Court seems more appropriate to a legislative judgment than a judicial one; (2c) the drafters of the Fourteenth Amendment did not intend to withdraw from the states the power to legislate with respect to abortion, and many state laws against abortion were not voided at that time; and (3) the Texas statute was struck down in toto even though the Court conceded that abortion during later stages of pregnancy could be restricted.

In a later abortion case, the 1992 case of *Planned Parenthood of Southeastern Pennsylvania v. Casey*, perhaps realizing the constitutional dubiousness of a foundation of privacy in its abortion jurisprudence, the Court sought either to broaden the privacy foundation of *Roe* or replace it with a more general individual liberty foundation. The Court stated in *Casey*:

> Constitutional protection of the woman's decision to terminate her pregnancy derives from the Due Process Clause of the Fourteenth Amendment. It declares that no State shall 'deprive any person of life, liberty, or property, without due process of law.' The controlling word in the cases before us is 'liberty.'

The Court then proceeded to work its way toward a definition of *liberty* without precedent:

> Our obligation is to define the liberty of all, not to mandate our own moral code... At the heart of liberty is the right to define one's own concept of existence, of the universe, of meaning, and the mystery of human life.

After such a definition as this, it would seem that there are no constraints on defining a concept of existence. How wide an invitation is this? Can anyone really define existence any way they want whenever they want? Where is this right in the Constitution and what would be the consequence if someone were to push this invitation beyond abortion?

On the Resolution of Moral Questions

It is a mistake to make a pretense of looking to the Constitution to resolve controversial moral questions such as abortion. The Constitution does not declare what is universally and necessarily right and good; it was never intended by its authors to do such a thing. The Supreme Court should recognize that it may sometimes find headed its way questions for which the Constitution is silent and defer them to the sovereign people. It should not try to find something in the Constitution that is not there. At the same time, it will not do to amend the Constitution to resolve controversial moral questions. If there is no perception by an individual that a certain question has moral dimensions, nothing as remote as a parchment, a legislature, or a collection of judges is likely to persuade that person about those dimensions, especially when the questions are perceived to not involve harm to someone else or involve one's own body. Experience with prohibition in the 1920s under the Eighteenth Amendment, which later ended up having to be repealed by the Twenty-First Amendment, is a chief example and lesson—the lawless disrespect endured by the Constitution. Nothing is gained by making the Constitution a weapon to resolve moral issues.

There is one point that may be drawn from the Eighteenth and Twenty-First amendments though that should not be missed. At least with these two amendments, the language of the Constitution was important; it was thought necessary to revise the language to make the Constitution say what, in each instance, the amendment ratifiers thought it should say. It is an entirely different matter when the Constitution is regarded as "a living document," the interpretation of which is subject to "the times." A living document mentality leads, even if in innocuous increments, toward the absurdity of the Constitution becoming unconstitutional. Respect for language is absent. Fortunately, disrespect for language can be returned to sender: interpretations by living document judges may be looked upon as similarly living. If the language of the Constitution is up for liberal interpretations, then so are the Supreme Court's dissertations.

The United States Constitution is treasured by many to be far and away the best system of governance ever devised by human wisdom. That it has not always been sufficient to restrain its circumvention for political expediency or to mediate conflicts of a moral nature does not detract from it. It is true that the Anti-Federalists have been dead right on a number of their criticisms, but it is probable that there was little that either the Federalists, the Anti-Federalists, or anyone else could have done (aside from a few of the subsequent amendments) or could do now to improve it. The Constitution has earned a place of honor; it has achieved in ample measure all of the things its preamble said it should achieve, and many of our best have fought and died upholding it. So if courts want their opinions to be honored, they should resist the temptation to rule according to the times and instead honor that which is honored by appealing to it in such a way as to bring it honor.

CHAPTER 3

THE WALL

I contemplate with sovereign reverence that act of the whole American people which declared that their legislature should 'make no law respecting an establishment of religion, or prohibiting the free exercise thereof,' thus building a wall of separation between church and state.

—**Thomas Jefferson**

Alliance, Then Separation

The snippet of the history of Western civilization straddling the eighth and ninth centuries and concurrent with the reigns of Pope Leo III and the Carolingian emperor Charles the Great is as good a candidate as any for being called the pinnacle of the alliance between church and state. Pope Leo III famously crowned Charles (also known as Charlemagne) as emperor in the year 800, sealing the concept of the divine right of kings. As kings considered their authority divinely warranted, for subjects to hold religious beliefs contrary to those of the king was viewed dimly at best, often as rebellion. The Roman emperor Theodosius had, in AD 380, decreed that everyone believe as the bishop of Rome (the pope) believed. Charles furthered the cause of religious uniformity in Western Europe with even greater precision. To Old World rulers, homogeny of belief was a chief means of eliminating challenges to their authority and preserving public order and stability. Religious dissent and deviation were often vigorously suppressed by civil authority. This was as much seen in earlier suppression of

Christianity by emperors of Rome in their upholding of paganism as in later suppression of deviations from Catholicism. Though persecution of Christians ceased after the ascension of Constantine to the emperorship in AD 312, containment of intellectual liberty and enforcement of doctrinal uniformity within Christianity began. Church and civil authority existed in a constant struggle as to which would oversee the other, but on the whole, both church and rulers were pleased with the arrangement: The church lent divine legitimacy to civil authority while civil authority prevented competition for the church. No religious liberty to be seen here.

As mentioned in chapter 1, fragmentation of religious authority resulting from the sixteenth century Protestant movements initially did little to crack state-enforced religious uniformity; the religion of the ruler remained the religion of the state: *Cujus regio, ejus religio* (whose realm, his religion). An escape from Old World church-state oppressions of conscience was found in the New World. But church-state thinking shadowed migrations to North America, even as the migrations moved beyond church-state reach. Inhabitants of colonial America were well invested in Old World religious traditions that had never been disassociated from political traditions. The Puritan colony of Massachusetts Bay exhibited no distinction between church and state. Most of the other colonies were founded with an officially authorized, state supported church, whether Anglican, Dutch Reformed, Catholic, or Quaker. Each colonial assembly, governor, and governor's council clung to their own particular brand of church.

In time, however, an effect of the Old World concept of church-state alliance deposited in the New World was to contribute to its own rapid dissolution. The legacy of constrained belief was such that it was possible for the Continental Congress to issue a public appeal to certain then common-place ideas—ideas harbored, in fact, under that legacy but soon to be found contrary to it. Those common place ideas were that (1) all men are created… by a particular creator, not a natural process; (2) all men are created equal in the sense of being equally free to act and equally in command of their actions; and (3) all men are endowed by that creator with certain unalienable rights associated with the freedom to act. There was recognition that the sole purpose of government is to secure those rights. There was assent to "the Laws of Nature [laws of human nature as necessary standards of social and economic interaction, not scientific principles] and Nature's God." There was an appeal to the "Supreme Judge of the world" and to "divine Providence." These common-place ideas and phrases either emanate from Christianity or, as for the purpose of government, are compatible with it. All are found in the 1776 Declaration of Independence.

Today, references to the Creator in a public document would be regarded by many as objectionable violations of the separation between church and state. But then, no one was raising objections to such public acknowledgments of God. Deference to Christianity was customary, reference to the word of God—the Bible—familiar, and religious terms in the Declaration of Independence unprovocative.[1] The denominations themselves, while being more than just different names for the same thing, could be said to hold tightly, even if less than faithfully, to something in common, the Bible. The point is that a common religious outlook, chiefly involving Protestant forms of Christianity, existed and appeared secure. Thomas Jefferson (1743–1826), primary author of the Declaration, later referred to the authority under which the Declaration had advanced its principles and registered its complaints as the "harmonizing sentiments of the day."[2] Most critically, even though it had long been entangled with political rule by considerations more suited to politics than religion, the religious outlook itself did not hinder the advance of the ideals of equality, liberty, and rights. Rather, the common religious viewpoint undergirded that advance and the quest for independence, a point obvious from the above referenced content of the Declaration of Independence.

Whatever one may think of their religious component now, the harmonizing sentiments were well discerned and expressed by Jefferson and the Continental Congress in the Declaration of Independence. Those sentiments also produced a most singular event for the cause of liberty in world history, the American Revolution. In addition to clarifying the case for independence, the Declaration spurred a few internal adjustments. A first and immediate one involved removal of the incongruity between mandatory taxation in support of religion and the liberty from taxation without consent being demanded by the colonies from the government of England. Why should any colony or the nation as a whole so protesting, turn and require the payment of taxes to support a religious establishment from a group in dissent? In nearly all recent instances, dissenters had been granted exemptions, but even the mere administration of exemptions by civil magistrates was an affront to the ideal of religious liberty.

Thus, in the spirit of separation and in front of the Virginia legislature in 1785, James Madison (1751–1836) could argue vociferously against a proposal by Patrick Henry (1736–99) for a tax to support the Commonwealth's various churches.[3] One's duty in matters of religion, including whether one should observe any duty at all, must, he contended, be directed by reason and conscience, not by civil magistrates. A civil magistrate cannot be a competent judge of religious truth. The right to believe as one chooses is reciprocal, meaning that anyone who asserts freedom to believe or not believe for one's self cannot deny the same to someone else. The duty toward one's creator precedes in time and exceeds in degree any claim on the individual from civil society. And if the duty of the individual in matters of religion already cannot be interceded or abridged by civil society, much less, then, by a legislature. It did not matter how small such a tax might be. A small tax would differ from the worst church-state abuses only in degree, he asserted. The effect of an earmarked tax on behalf of churches, he went on, is state authorized churches' lack of vitality and an admission that they cannot be sustained on their own merits. It would further serve to deter immigrants seeking refuge from the evils of state religions elsewhere, incline present inhabitants to emigrate, and aggravate inter-denominational "animosities and jealousies."[4]

The record of state-established religions is that they have never been guardians of liberty but consistently desire to achieve uniformity and suppress dissenting views. Religion is an excellent tool for the state to regulate and correct opinion, never minding that the religion may be distorted, even becoming unrecognizable in the process. Wherever an entanglement exists between government and religion, it is certain to lead to corruption of both: a religious state gains license to oppress in the name of religious truth and a state religion gains the means to remove competition. On these points, Madison was right in insisting on a decisive separation between government and religion. Henry's concern was the backing that Christianity supplied to civic virtue. His desire to see a means of maintaining that virtue and the continuity of the then existing religious worldview, considering its fatherly presence in the Declaration, was equally laudable. It is certainly the case that a uniformity of religious views cannot be sustained indefinitely solely by its own inertia. He considered that something more was necessary. It was just that there needed to be found some other means than government and taxation to do it.

Once the common cause of revolution united the colonies under the Articles of Confederation, competitive denominational spirits vying for status as the national religion were put aside; there was to be no national denomination. Thus, it was church-state separation, perhaps as much or more than other ideals of liberty written into the first entry of the Bill of Rights a few years later, that would grace the dignity of the newly independent nation.[5] To the aid of Henry's concern, precedents and traditions long established do not immediately go to pieces when original factors in their adoption are withdrawn. Church-state separation was declared and practiced while the congruity of belief and the benefits of that congruity persisted. The post-declaration surge of church-state separations and declarations of religious liberty within the states were a sign of unity—unity around the principle of religious liberty—not an immediate cause of disunity. While religious liberty was deemed a necessity because of the multiplicity of denominations, a harmony of understanding about God, the universe, human nature, the meaning of life, and a just and prosperous society remained. The one exception, the one multiculturalism, involved a division over slavery, the resolution and associated adjustment of which were deferred.

It is not so unusual to see harmonizing sentiments unravel. Today, the dissolution is evident in the introduction and proliferation of more and more diversity in beliefs and worldviews, particularly in diverging views on justice, the proper role of government, and what ought to be encompassed as individual rights. Although there were divergences within Christianity in the founding era of the United

States, divergence from its worldview was miniscule. This point and the context it enfolded around the Declaration of Independence and the First Amendment to the Constitution must be admitted a place in the historic backdrop. The effect of the prior coercive church-state alliance greatly encompassed the founders' world, and they could hardly have imagined a condition of its absence even as they rightly strove to break free of it. The irony is that the circumstance of religion at the founding, as much as it had been fashioned by centuries upon centuries of compulsion, became a key element in the appeal for religious liberty. There were enough variations in its forms to make a unitary national religion impossible yet sufficient unity among the variations to form a shared basis of appeal. That appeal was first for independence, but it also quickly supplied the reasoning for church-state separation. So now, what about the consequences of diverging belief systems seen today, a divergence that the founding statesmen/authors could hardly have anticipated?

Undercurrents of Metaphysical Anarchy

The steps toward attainment of individual sovereignty in matters of belief and the separation of church and state have been among the greatest strands in the history of Western civilization. The record of the achievement does not suggest a trajectory guided by some overarching plan, however. Not only were there frequent setbacks and retractions involving reappearances of coercive attempts to control belief, there were other historical strands simultaneously and subtly working against freedom of conscience and the gains of church-state separation. These other strands would eventually produce a sort of *power game* over belief and religion.

In conventional wisdom, the contributions to liberty by the scientific revolution of the seventeenth century (freeing knowledge from religious authority) and by the Enlightenment era of the eighteenth century (freeing governance from religious sanction) are seen to be as great or greater than those of any other historical periods. Christianity in name, though less in spirit, had steered Western civilization down a crooked path. While many of the liberties enjoyed in the modern West, such as those of the Magna Carta, descended from developments of the medieval ages when institutional religion ruled heavily, it is true that religious liberty was not one of them. Freedom was now to be found in breaking free from the religious mold. Science began to see its success in the power of rational inference explode; religion began to see an imperialistic science outmatch its intellectual resources. Here was nothing less than a transfer of cultural authority from religion to science, finding root in these two centuries.

The problem is that science is pretty useless in judging what is right and good. Reason without faith in some final justice is equally useless as a restraint against the darker aspects of human nature. Reason, in fact, often ends up in service to darker aspects, justifying their particular emergences. Reasonings are crafted to cover ethical slipups. Questionable means are presumed to be justified by the goals they achieve. Science and reason are poor substitutes for the metaphysical6 premises traditionally associated with the discernment between right and wrong and between good and evil. In their displacing of metaphysical premises, rightness and goodness become cultural and even individual selections, which they tend to become anyway, but without metaphysical backing, only more so. After all, who wants to run up against reasons for not doing what they want to do? The trend has reached its full extent and is perhaps best described by the sophomoric shriek, "Who are you to impose your beliefs on me!" Well, granted, this exclamation is entirely consistent with individual sovereignty in matters of belief and separation between church and state. Do sovereignty and separation leave anything more than the defiance that nothing is right or good except "what I decide"? As much as the secular template for the state makes religion a non-participant in matters of public interest, who can say on a scientific platform that anything one might think or want to do is not right and good?

How human beings came to be actuated by a sense of rightness, goodness, and justice is not at all clear to the scientific mind. Is it environment and upbringing and thus instilled? Or is it genetic and thereby instinctive? Is it reasoned and thereby possibly objective? Or is it intuitive, immediately apprehended and understood without the conscious use of reasoning? Or is it a recipe involving all these? One thing is known beyond any doubt: no form of religion is necessary to have the sense. Whether they maintain religious beliefs or not, everyone is acutely aware of wrong and injustice, especially when wrongs and injustices are directed at themselves. The sense of right and wrong, good and evil, justice and injustice is both a blessing and a curse. First, it is a blessing; its absence would leave persons little more than flotsam and jetsam in the ocean of their existence. There would be scant motivation to secure the right, the good, or the just because right, good, and just would be empty concepts. However, its presence means continual conflict over the propriety of words and actions and indignation over even the slightest infraction. It is a dread in the quest to escape condemnation yet a delight in sticking condemnation on others, thereby elevating one's self-rightness.

If the sense of rightness, goodness, and justice is an imprint of the supernatural on, say, conscience, the supernatural may still be denied while the imprint remains operative. But if the sense is not implanted supernaturally, how does it arise? Is it accidental? Is it somehow a consequence of laws of nature? Why is it unique to human beings? Whatever the why and how, it does not seem to be a simple matter of programming or reprogramming. What exactly is the nature of the resistance to reformulating or reinventing morality anyway? We will not lose sight of these questions as we proceed. For now, though, let us continue to follow the undercurrents.

The secular state, in addition to being the apparent logical consequence of church-state separation, is nowadays also undergirded by scientific naturalism. Scientific naturalism centers on the belief that science has disproven the supernatural. Originally, scientific naturalism was a stipulation, an agreement among scientists to restrict scientific investigation to natural causes to explain natural phenomena and to exclude supernatural causes. Now it is advanced as if it were a conclusion, that natural causes are all that exist. Having slipped that deception past an unsuspecting public, it is not a huge step to then apportion to science the entire domain of rationality. Thus, all religions with any hint of supernatural content are categorized as non-rational, and as non-rational, there are no rational grounds for comparison. Here, then, arrives pluralization—a plurality of religious views, the idea that no religion is truer, or more "correctly" less false, than another. Choosing between religions becomes somewhat like choosing between different flavors of ice cream—the criteria are subjective, preferential, typically cultural, and never objective or universal. With that, the utility of reason in metaphysical inquiries falls away.

Once reason is sufficiently distanced from it, metaphysical reality becomes experiential, no longer propositional. Here, then, arrives privatization. Facts, such as the facts of science, can be admitted into the public domain as public resources but not subjective personal preferences. These are to be kept private. So if religion is personal spiritual experience and not propositional truth, it becomes a private matter. Therefore, "Keep your religion to yourself!" The same applies to your values.

Secularization, pluralization, and privatization7 have shut down the possibility of reasoned metaphysical inquiry in the minds of people everywhere. They have imposed upon persons an unnatural division into public and private halves—that is, a prohibition against publicly appealing to any origin for the sense of rightness, goodness, and justice outside of themselves. Yet it is a shared sense that rules the public domain. What are laws but "thou shalts" and "thou shalt nots" according to a shared understanding of what is right, good, and just? Secularization, pluralization, and privatization would seem to be producing a state of metaphysical anarchy, not at all a sustaining force for harmonizing sentiments.

The Power Game Threat to Consent and Natural Right

Science and reason are suited to the role of method and process, not the fashioning of premises. But in their overreach, supposing to have invalidated metaphysical or supernatural points of reference, they have mistakenly invented for themselves a naturalistic premise. It is not a good one for them. Scientific reasoning, non-material as it is, must exist outside of the material cause-effect world. It cannot be admitted as a material cause-effect inevitability without raising a question as to its status as an instrument of truth.

As this point is unrecognized, scientific naturalism as a religion of sorts has slipped into the position of state religion. Its supremacy is reinforced in public education and mass media. The wall of separation between church and state was never a barrier to scientific naturalism; it does not look, sound, or feel like religion. However, there is no neutrality. Religion is going to have to include scientific naturalism and secularism if they are going to be counted as alternatives to other forms of it. "Ah, but they are counted as the absence of religion, not religious alternatives," they say. Very well then, but what happens in the absence of the traditional platform of rightness, goodness, and justice?

There should not be any ignorance as to the theoretical problem presented by this question. The seeming legitimate appeal to secular-scientific neutrality is, as noted, empty of rightness, goodness, and justice. Neither secularism nor scientific naturalism has any ethical or moral content of its own. The content has to be obtained from something else. Moral content obtained from something else becomes as much a religion as any other. Of course, it is never a case of having to invent ethical and moral content from scratch where no content has existed before, nor does the refusal of a metaphysical platform for right and good mean an immediate degradation of justice. The moral landscape is still abundantly sign-posted by conscience and an innate or intuitive grasp of the right and good. Metaphysical roots may indeed be denied recognition while still present and operative. Nevertheless, as anarchy or the absence of government is an unsettled political state leaving justice without an overseer, so is the absence of a basis of appeal for social order or everyone doing what is right in their own eyes.[8] The two conditions are hardly distinguishable. In either case, it is an intolerable state over which someone will attempt to take charge. Widely accepted denial of the natural root of justice invites a substitute. Now one may begin to get a hint of the problem and how the rigidly secular state may flirt with tyranny as much as any religious state.

In the quest to clamp down on anarchy of thought and belief and conform public sentiments to specific priorities or agendas, ample use has been made of tyrannical oppression. Religions, whether invented or commandeered, have also served as instruments of conformity. One of these seems to be taking a more and more aggressive role toward that end in certain regions of the world today and is one which has historically also been among the more aggressive.[9] The atheistic political ideologies of communism and socialism were invented more recently, but the record of the last century is quite sufficient for everyone to see what they have routinely done to individual rights. Characteristic of atheistic ideologies is that their materialist basis is threatened by religion. They must be well fortified against any avenue originating external to their dominions that might offer hope, and which hope might possibly be turned against them. This they do through heavy-handed suppression or regulation. But atheistic ideologies, in their suppression of religion, effectively take religion's place and thereby become just another form of it. Whether it is a this-worldly utopian state religion or a materialistic utopian state with religious fervor, it is all directed toward the control of thought and belief.

In an otherwise free society, control of thought and belief is possible too. Though this must at first be driven through non-governmental channels and without associated precepts becoming law, the limitation is not a terrible handicap. When once metaphysical backing is driven away, moral coordinates are portrayed as possessing a different nature. Instead of being universal and unchangeable, they are pitched as customary, conventional, or preferential arrangements determined by social factors—typically labeled as social contracts, that is, whatever everyone seems to agree to. Morality and ethics are perceived to be what culture has by custom or convention or what a majority of individuals have by preference or whatever sentiments seem to have the most popular appeal or whatever seems expedient. The criterion for right and good becomes pragmatic and utilitarian. It is reminiscent of the two political philosophies of the same names (see Appendix A). Under these suppositions, boundaries between good and evil are open to being redrawn and what is set before the public in education, news, entertainment, music, art, literature, and theatre fashions the public's sentiments. If certain aspects of morality are consistently portrayed as overdue for revision, popular opinion about them will, sooner or later as it seems, swing accordingly.

Many want to play this game—that is, the selective ditching of moral coordinates so as to replace them with others. They believe that is freedom. Freedom is not found in self-restraint, but rather in its opposite. Self-restraint is, to them, idiocy. Why not adjust morality to desire rather than adjust desire to morality? Be certain of this: the resulting parade of appetites is not going to be satisfied with an absence of consent to its agenda. The necessary consent will be produced by coercion. Here, then, enters the use of power where the propaganda and surgical procedure of political correctness is applied to the "collective" conscience. In order to bring about these sorts of adjustments in a free society, everyone must be re-educated to accept the more "advanced" set of moral coordinates or else be edited out of public discourse. The form of correctness becomes political, not objective and transcendent, and note that it is "correctness" and not "goodness" as "political goodness" would be a conjunction of discordant terms. Resolutions of moral questions become an elimination of competitors in a sort of political "survival of the most aggressive" power contest. In this, values get shoved back into the public domain after having been supposedly stashed away in the private. Secularization supplies the opportunity to reshape "less favorable," "outdated," or "intolerant" moral and ethical content around some other ground for it—exacting measures of inter-group equality and reworked boundaries of toleration perhaps. In this, the pursuit of happiness becomes more communal than individual, rolling over the yet unpersuaded in its surge. Political correctness power gamers have no hesitation about doing this. Their tactic is the same as the one they war against—moral condemnation. Moral condemnation is a powerful instrument. More than advanced weaponry or the global economy, to gain control over morality may be the ultimate power high.

If less than upright reasonings or, to borrow again James Madison's phrase from Federalist 63, "the artful misrepresentations of interested men" can be marshaled to serve darker aspects of humanity once, then they can be marshaled to do so again. But most relentless is the logic of a condition without fixed moral coordinates. Under that condition, there is nothing to which more honest appeal may gravitate. Something is needed to rescue reason from a weightless condition, or we all become captive to the manipulations and intimidations of cultural gatekeepers seeking to sanctify their "superior" morality. C.S. Lewis pinpoints the problem:

> If *good* means only the local ideology, how can those who invent the local ideology be guided by any idea of good themselves? The very idea of freedom presupposes some objective moral law which overarches rulers and ruled alike. Subjectivism about values is eternally incompatible with democracy. We and our rulers are of one kind only so long as we are subject to one law. But if there is no Law of Nature, the *ethos* of any society is the creation of its rulers, educators, and conditioners; and every creator stands above and outside his own creation.[10]

Such "creators" are always anxious to complete their program. Consent of the governed and the natural rights of conscience and speech are never in so much peril as when the creators assume a role that would otherwise have been reserved for God.

From Land to Faith

If natural right and consent of the governed were once held in high awareness as pillars of liberty, another necessity may be as much underappreciated. It is worthy of a momentary detour. North America was the last livable continent to be explored. Not much more than 200 years ago, no one knew the extent of its vastness, least of all the native inhabitants. It seems unlikely that the continent could have remained mostly unknown so long into the march of civilization, but it was. To overlook the role of North America in establishing the conditions of liberty would be to suggest that American liberty could have happened anywhere. Obviously, it did not. The abundance of unsettled land and the opportunity it presented for the pursuit of happiness were indispensable. That opportunity continued generation after generation, from the colonial period into the early twentieth century.[11] Continual westward migration always exceeded the geographic reach of established government. The possibility of a better existence was always available on the generally blank left side of the map, if one could overcome the challenges and dangers. By this, self-reliance and self-governance were driven into the American conscience, even if as much in myth as reality. The North American interior West idealizes liberty in its vastness, openness, ruggedness, still much unsubdued landscape, distant horizons, and in its risk, danger, opportunity, and physical elevation—it is not low country. The remaining tracts of publicly owned land in the interior West allow one an opportunity to experience some sense of that same freedom and independence even if only for brief periods.

The experience of self-reliance and self-governance produced an acute awareness and zeal for liberty quite apart from any constitutional principles. American liberty has doubtless been associated with virtues of self-reliance and self-governance in times past, and it would have been unimaginable for one to not be accompanied by the other. But now if liberty sprang from these virtues, does it require them? Nowadays, with more and more intrusive government redistribution of wealth producing widespread dependency, what is the effect on self-reliance? What is the probability that anyone would refuse an overbearing government on which depends their livelihood? The answer and its consequences for liberty should be obvious, and no more will be said about it. Perhaps less obvious, with most educational institutions teaching that metaphysical beliefs are non-rational and subjective, leaving virtue and moral uprightness without its traditional root, what is the effect on self-governance?

Few observations about human nature are as obvious as the need to restrain it. A difficulty arises with this observation though because it is also human nature to think that it is everyone else that needs restraining, and that one's own impulses are perfectly justified. Nevertheless, people cannot always do whatever they please if they want to remain free. Thus, British statesman Edmund Burke (1729 -97) wrote in 1791:

> Men are qualified for civil liberty in exact proportion to their disposition to put moral chains upon their own appetites; in proportion as their love to justice is above their

rapacity; in proportion as their soundness and sobriety of understanding is above their vanity and presumption; in proportion as they are more disposed to listen to the counsels of the wise and good, in preference to the flattery of knaves. Society cannot exist unless a controlling power upon will and appetite be placed somewhere, and the less of it there is within, the more there must be without. It is ordained in the eternal constitution of things, that men of intemperate minds cannot be free.[12]

Liberty, according to Burke, requires self-control or internal restraint—self-governance. If internal restraint is lacking, restraint defaults to external, and liberty is, of course, inconsistent with external restraint.

With similar perception, French political observer Alexis Charles Henri Maurice Clerel de Tocqueville (1805–59) wrote to a friend:

> To persuade men that respect for the laws of God and man is the best means of remaining free, and that liberty is the best means of remaining upright and religious cannot, you say, be done. I too am tempted to think so. But the thing is true, all the same, and I will try to say so at all costs.[13]

Tocqueville was aware of the difficulty of instilling respect for law—law as something applicable to one's self as much as everyone else. Respect for law cannot be forced; it is an internally generated restraint and, he says consistent with Burke, "The best means of remaining free." If such respect and associated internal restraint can be made self-perpetuating, a state of liberty may endure. Continual disrespect for law and misuse of freedom generates demand for external restraint, which invariably is restraint by government. Fear of penalty is no substitute for respect and generally only drives violations and misuse out of sight.

Restraint is unlikely to long survive under rules that individuals make up for themselves; they will adjust their rules rather than stand perpetually against desires that oppose them. But no one gets to make up all their own rules. Restraint against inflicting harm is the minimum; objectivity of the injunction against inflicting harm is a tacit exception even among a morally relativistic population. The very use of the term *corrections* as in *The Department of Corrections* (the administration of jails) presupposes at least some well-established coordinates as to what is right, good, and just. If Burke and Tocqueville are right, if freedom requires internal restraint of human nature, then some mechanism besides human nature itself must be available to do that. Whatever the mechanism, it is well for the cause of liberty that it has very little to do with departments of corrections.

The mechanism the founders identified is the traditional one and not a surprise. What the virtue of self-governance requires is faith. Faith supplies the motivation to continue in virtue, even when it does not appear advantageous at the moment. Without faith that virtue is rewarded, self-restraint too easily crumbles when no one is monitoring it or when one's livelihood or plans might be hindered by its practice. One's motivation may further drop onto the lower platform of self-indulgence, which is an invitation to corruption, moral defacement, fraud, and thievery. In contrast, liberty, the founders often asserted, requires virtue, and virtue requires faith. In reference to these points, author Os Guinness expounds on what he calls the golden triangle of freedom.[14] The triangle has three points connected by three sides. The points are virtue, faith, and liberty. Each side is a dependency. The first side is that liberty depends on or requires virtue; the second is that virtue requires faith. The third side of the triangle is that faith requires liberty, specifically the religious liberty found in the disestablishment and free exercise of religion as encoded in the First Amendment. Faith is not to be outlawed, restricted, or regulated by government. So the triangle is faith leading to virtue then to liberty and back to faith.

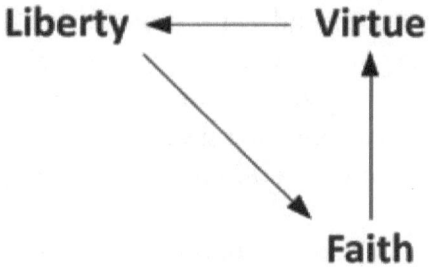

American founders and statesmen of the late eighteenth century repeatedly affirmed the principles represented in the triangle. Following is a sample of their words on the topic.

> Only a virtuous people are capable of freedom. As nations become corrupt and vicious, they have more need of masters.[15]
>
> —Signer of the Declaration of Independence and the Constitution,
> Benjamin Franklin (1706–90)

> The only foundation for a useful education in a republic is to be laid in religion. Without this there can be no virtue, and without virtue there can be no liberty, and liberty is the object and life of all republican governments.[16]
>
> —Signer of the Declaration of Independence,
> Benjamin Rush (1746–1813)

> Of all the dispositions and habits which lead to political prosperity, religion and morality are indispensable supports… And let us with caution indulge the supposition that morality can be maintained without religion… Whatever may be conceded to the influence of refined education… reason and experience both forbid us to expect that national morality can prevail in exclusion of religious principle… It is substantially true that virtue or morality is a necessary spring of popular government…

The rule indeed extends with more or less force to every species of free government...Let it be simply asked, where is the security for property, for reputation, for life, if the sense of religious obligation desert the oaths which are the instruments of investigation in the courts of justice?

—Commander of the Continental Army,
Presider over the Constitutional Convention,
and first President of the United States,
George Washington (1732–99) from the *Farewell Address*

We have no government armed with power capable of contending with human passions unbridled by morality and religion... Our Constitution was made only for a moral and religious people. It is wholly inadequate to the government of any other.[17]

—Signer of the Declaration of Independence,
John Adams (1735–1826)

To suppose that any form of government will secure liberty or happiness without any virtue in the people, is a chimerical idea.[18]

—Signer of the Constitution,
James Madison (1751–1836)

Neither the wisest constitution nor the wisest laws will secure the liberty and happiness of a people whose manners are universally corrupt... He therefore is the truest friend to the liberty of his country who tries most to promote its virtue.[19]

—Signer of the Declaration of Independence,
Samuel Adams (1722–1803)

The politician who loves liberty, sees them [scenes of the pillage and slaughter of the French Revolution] with regret as a gulf that may swallow up the liberty to which he is devoted. He knows that [with] morality overthrown (and morality must fall with religion), the terrors of despotism can alone curb the impetuous passions of man, and confine him within the bounds of social duty.[20]

—Signer of the Constitution,
Alexander Hamilton (1755–1804)

Bad men cannot make good citizens. It is impossible that a nation of infidels or idolaters should be a nation of free men. It is when a people forget God, that tyrants forge their chains. A vitiated state of morals, a corrupted public conscience, is incompatible with freedom.[21]

—Preeminent American Patriot,
Patrick Henry (1736–99)

Even the most deistic of the founders, Benjamin Franklin and Thomas Jefferson, acknowledged the relevance of divine providence. Franklin had proposed at one point during the 1787 Constitutional Convention to begin each day with prayer; Jefferson was the primary author of the Declaration of Independence with its "firm reliance on the protection of divine Providence."

Contrary to much criticism they endure in regard to their failure to eradicate slavery, the founders were honorable men. Their most insolent critics have no concept of the difficulties involved in getting rid of an entrenched culture and system of labor that continued to be profitable. The founders were under immense pressure to deal with issues of independence and national unity. Abrupt abandonment of slavery would have caused (and eventually did cause) a great deal of economic, social, and political turmoil in the short-run, turmoil that, if concurrent to the revolution and constitutional framing, would doubtless have been catastrophic for independence and national unity.

What is most important in referencing the founder's words is to figure out why what they said is true. If civic education was taken seriously, it should not be necessary to appeal to their words. It would be known already why what they said is true. A chief purpose of this book, therefore, is to recover the necessary understanding that informs the founders thinking, not just to take them at their word.

The best leaders move beyond self-reliance and self-governance, setting aside self-interest for the common good. If no one in the past had worked for the common good, the common would not be good and the good would not be common. Under pressure of the moment, right and good seem always at a disadvantage to deceit and treachery. Corruption is endemic in government. Those in power too often strive to acquire more and more of it and misuse it for self-serving ends. Leaders who would stand for the right and good against corruption must be assured, in the face of much evidence to the contrary, that they will prevail in the end. The good includes preservation of liberty, the securing of individual rights, which is the sole purpose of government. It was at personal cost that the best leaders founded the nation or steered it through some of its most difficult periods. American citizens should know who their best leaders have been. It should not be necessary to mention them by name. What does need to be mentioned is that the self-sacrifice they exhibited required even more faith, faith that was not just willy-nilly something fashionable to fill up the space in the mind allocated for beliefs. A legitimacy and authenticity would seem necessary for faith to persist through resistance and opposition, when the end goal would otherwise appear at present to not be worth all the trouble.

In view of this point about leadership, there is an aspect to the triangular concept of freedom that the founders seem not to have considered. It seems probable that the prior alliance between church and state had obscured awareness of its absence: the faith requires liberty side of the triangle puts no accountability on faith. I would venture, therefore, an augmentation of the triangle. I would make it into a square by inserting reason in between faith and liberty. Faith requires reason. Faith might be left alone to pursue happy delusions were it not for the fact that beliefs have consequences which may burst out into the public ear and eye via speech and action. Whether for good or for evil, beliefs cannot be expected to remain forever dormant or benign. Because there are connections between belief and speech and between belief and action, faith cannot be left entirely a private matter. Therefore, to the end that beliefs might not be anarchic, aimlessly diverging from a harmony of sentiment or veering toward misrepresentations of reality and human nature that could detract from a state of liberty, reason must be free to set forth its arguments and evidence assessing the truthfulness of faith—in public.

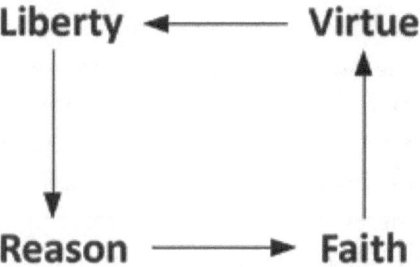

The need for inserting reason to put a check on faith is straightforward. There is an indirect threat to liberty from a lack of well-reasoned, confident faith and a consequent failure to uphold public virtue. But there is more. There is a further threat to liberty not imminently menacing at the time of the founding: if able to be misdirected, faith can be made a tool useful for social control. It is because religion, in one form or another, inhabits the public domain. As much as one form would be walled out, another sneaks in. The peril to a state of liberty in the absence of an understanding of this point is real. Whether it is the seduction of a utopian ideology, the self-righteousness of an invented or commandeered religion, or the smug ascendency of scientific naturalism, secularism, and political religion, communal beliefs and goals are able to beguile and captivate a majority. These beliefs and goals then supply the basis on which power agendas work moral condemnation to their advantage. That is, they work moral condemnation by controlling belief—not by eliminating religion, rather, by aligning it with collective agendas. What is believed communally about reality and human nature forms the basis on which moral condemnation obtains its power. How this is done will be more specifically brought out in chapter 5.

Should power gamers succeed in working moral condemnation to the advantage of communal goals that they define, the public agenda may be preempted, and once preempted, individual rights are easily displaced. The need to thwart this maneuver is continual. If virtue and reason are extraneous to communal goals (and they usually are extraneous to those that beguile and captivate), they drop out of the formula, and the square of liberty dissolves. Wayward beliefs about reality and human nature, then, must be subjected to some measure of truth. The freedom of speech, particularly free course given to religious and political argument, may constitute the most vital necessity for a state of liberty to endure. It is reason, more so than faith that requires liberty. Whatever reasoning may be out there, one may still choose to believe in whatever one wants, anytime one wants, and wherever one wants. Reason requires liberty because critical assessments of cultural conditioning, popular propaganda, and trendy tirades may be unfavorably received. Offense may be taken at critiques of the less than defendable. Offense and disfavor are what generate the Holy Office, the gulag, politically correct journalism, and uncountable numbers of other attempts to regulate thought.

Liberty requires virtue. Virtue requires faith. Faith requires reason. Reason requires liberty. The square is not holding up well. Centuries of academic arrogance and spinelessness have left faith and reason at opposite ends of the universe. Even in the era of the founding, faith was being artificially partitioned from reason—the result of the science versus religion wrangle. More recently, the founders' faith to virtue connection has been unhitched; the one "virtue" elevated today seems to be hesitancy to insert one's faith into the public ear, especially if one's faith should happen to be Christianity. Unrestrained self-indulgence is mistaken as liberty; it is now a right to coddle any amusement. And the liberty to reason in defense of faith is ignored or suppressed. This last point may be verified by walking into most any university and offering to present a reasoned case for Christianity. With all four of the sides of this square of liberty being contested or denied in today's world, religious liberty, if not liberty in general, may now be just so much water circling the drain. North America once supplied an opportunity for the possibilities of political liberty to be realized. Habitable, non-jurisdictional, and unsettled land to restore those possibilities may not ever become available again.

Reasoned Pathways to Convergence?

The postmodern injunction to "not impose your values on anyone else" is an assertion with moral content; it is *wrong* to impose values on someone else. It would appear that they believe everything should be tolerated. Yet they are blind to the fact of their own moral impositioning and intolerance. Primarily, value neutrality is impossible; everyone operates according to what they regard as valuable—typically their own livelihood, the respect for which they are generally pleased to impose on everyone else. Value noncommitalism (the refusal to commit to any values) is a position viable only in postmodern classrooms, not a resolution for the practical world. Regardless of how formulated, prioritizations of value are imposed. And they must be imposed; an administration of justice cannot exist without a prioritization. Values really do inhabit the public domain. If life has no value, then it is fine to murder or misuse it. We know that it does have value; that is the first unalienable right. All ordering of value and the administration of justice begin there.

Besides the absence of values being out of the question, agreement on value priorities is necessary. Diverging opinion on what is right, good, and just leads to civil disharmony, even violent conflict. Slavery was a divisive public matter. "A house divided against itself cannot stand" was the descriptive metaphor drawn from the words of Jesus by Abraham Lincoln on the matter. It may be noted that among the Constitution's stated purposes are to "form a more perfect union, establish justice, [and] ensure domestic tranquility." Even in a secularized, pluralized, and otherwise privatized society, agreement in the public domain is sought for these very purposes. Balancing the necessity of agreement on value priorities and an administration of justice, however, liberty requires that reasoned persuasion and consent prevail, not coercion.

No one of an age able to reason and make rational decisions should be forced to comply with someone else's thought program. Coercion includes the subtle and corrosive effect of political correctness on independence of thought, freedom of inquiry, and reasoned debate. Reasoned persuasion is the only means of achieving agreement that respects each person's rationality and autonomy.

Against the need for reasoned persuasion, though, is the towering fact of raw intuition on questions of right and good. *Raw* is a fitting qualifier because how often does anyone ever question their intuition on such matters? Even while it is known neither by science nor philosophy precisely how individuals acquire their sense of right and good, as moral psychologist Jonathan Haidt notes, *intuitive* is the word that best seems to describe it.[22] Intuition is useless in persuasion. I cannot apply my intuition to persuade someone with a different intuition that it is their intuition that needs to be adjusted, not mine. Though it is desirable in the interest of liberty that reasoned arguments do the persuading to achieve agreement, they are not generally able to do that. If reason ever gets involved, it is invariably to justify what is felt intuitively or what satisfies one's appetites, not to set one's sense of right and good more aright.[23] Reasoned arguments cannot attain the immediacy and impress of intuition. Philosopher Bertrand Russell (1872–1970) wrote that while "social cohesion is a necessity… mankind has never yet succeeded in enforcing cohesion by merely rational arguments."[24] Madison's faction ridden populace would seem to confirm it. A potential mayhem of moral intuitions would seem to stand in the way of the Constitution's ends of union, justice, and tranquility.

Heightening the variability of moral intuition is the fact that no one is ever in a state of isolation from the beliefs and values of everyone else. Everyone issues moral commendations and condemnations. They do that because they know there is more to right than mere might; conscience is not satisfied with "might makes right." The knowledge of good and evil is too acute to be set aside. Though it may be insisted that the source of that knowledge should be found elsewhere, the inability to eradicate it is entirely consistent with a quality of innateness that would seem to have been gained in the

Garden of Eden. It is possible to distort, bend, suppress, manipulate, selectively apply, or feign ignorance of that knowledge but not to get rid of it. It is here that diverging views on right and good become evident. There is not quite enough rigidity to prevent manipulation. One way to not be found trespassing over the boundary between good and evil is by moving the boundary. Here, then, arises a distinction between distorting, bending, or suppressing the rules and violating them. It is only violations that send one back around to the necessity of an administration of justice, the discouraging of deviations from the rules by some form of judicial system. What shall be said about the rules themselves?

Legislatures are tasked to settle upon rules and courts are often accorded the final say. But legislatures and courts are not always able to resolve differences in moral intuition either. As much as legislature and court had tried to bridge the divergence of views over slavery, it had unfortunately to be resolved by war. It is quite certain that the controversy over abortion will never be settled by legislatures and courts. And there is no chance that a boundary for that could ever be drawn on a map. Much is left unanswered. The Constitution has forms in place that restrain governmental zeal and the bad effects of democracy. But controversies over what is right, good, and just remain and the power games proceed. The logic of a condition without fixed moral coordinates to which reasoned appeal may be directed is indeed relentless. Lack of moral coordinates leaves even constitutional government adrift and vulnerable to the "artful misrepresentations of interested men."

Even John Stuart Mill (1806–73), the nineteenth century author of the famed *On Liberty*, seems to have recognized this point, though it is most certainly not drawn out in that popular book—a book that argues against the coercion associated with moral injunctions whose violation causes no apparent harm to another:

> In all political societies which have had a durable existence, there has been some fixed point; something which men agreed in holding sacred; which it might or might not be lawful to contest in theory, but which no one

could either fear or hope to see shaken in practice; which, in short (except perhaps during some temporary crisis), was in the common estimation placed above discussion... But when the questioning of these fundamental principles is (not an occasional disease, but) the habitual condition of the body politic; and when all the violent animosities are called forth, which spring naturally from such a situation, the state is virtually in a position of civil war; and can never long remain free from it in act and fact.[25]

A hint as to the consequences of the presence or absence of fixed moral coordinates may be found in contrasting the two late eighteenth century revolutions, the American and the French. The American Revolution (1776–83) left established and sacred reference points including state religions and certain judicial elements of English constitutional heritage compatible with those religions undisturbed. The French Revolution (1789–99) attacked the established religion, having found it insufficiently distinct from all that was bad about the former royal state. It then sought to redefine good and evil in terms favorable to the new democratic state. The French Revolution at first announced commitment to liberte, egalite, fraternite (liberty, equality, fraternity). This was all well and good until liberty became the liberty of the state, not the individual. There was no check on the liberty of the state; its liberty was total. This was the ultimate power trip for those who could gain control, and control exchanged hands often until ending up in those of a tyrant who was wise about it: Napoleon. The American Revolution positioned the state as servant— servant to the sole end of securing the rights of individuals, as granted to them by their Creator. Contrast that with the novel and consequently insecure French Revolution, which proceeded to squash all dissent, chopping off heads in the elimination of threats to the well-being of the state. It then went on to consume even the revolution's own advocates suspected of treachery against those momentarily in power. The French Revolution failed to achieve its ideal of liberty for this reason: there was no inducement to public virtue that could withstand the paranoia of easily acquired power. Here was a hatchet job that set a pattern for many future revolutions of utopian-styled tyranny. The American Revolution left religion alone to fulfill its role of expressing the reality of the Creator in public affairs and produced the most stable form of liberty yet seen.

Liberty requires that government and those who assume positions as cultural gatekeepers are unable to manipulate the right, good, and just to their liking or to distort the unalienable rights. Only in a metaphysical, transcendent, or supernatural reality may an incorruptible law reside. In this, the wall of separation between church and state does not eliminate the relevance of valid truth claims of religion. And if the American system is the better system, it should be necessary to make space for them.

Summary Remarks

There are a few points pertaining to interactions between religion and government that must be credited as learned from history:

1. For the cause of freedom of conscience—that is, the freedom to follow one's conscience—the wall of separation between church and state must be a real barrier; it must prevent church and state from access to each other's billfolds and meeting rooms, from state control over church and church control over state.
2. The prime measure of a civilization is the liberty of its citizens, and the measure of liberty is the degree to which reasoned appeal is accommodated. Persuasion on matters of public interest, particularly those that also happen to be matters of conscience, must bow before consent and the opportunity to freely and openly agree or disagree.

However, the following further points drawn from what has been discussed so far should qualify a strict view of the wall of separation between church and state:

3. Appeal to the right, good, and just, and to unalienable individual rights, is effective only when these cannot be distorted, manipulated, or arbitrarily decreed. Laws can make legal and illegal. They cannot make right, good, or just, and they cannot invent rights.
4. Natural law notwithstanding, it is a mistake to think that reason alone will always settle onto the right, good, and just. Reason is generally unable to restrain passion or overtake intuition and invariably ends up as a tool to justify whatever deed is already being done or whatever assertion about justice is already believed. Something more is necessary.
5. Faith in a transcendence that backs rightness, goodness, and justice, including unalienable rights, is the one thing that can sustain the virtue necessary to resist and oppose the urge to distort, manipulate, or arbitrarily decree them. Being the assurance of what is not yet in sight or in hand, faith holds out for a better end.
6. If justice and rights are to be publicly secured against distortion, manipulation, and arbitrary decree, reasoned pathways to their true metaphysical habitation, wherever that may be, must be free to enter public discourse.
7. Suppression of reasoned pathways to the metaphysical by secularism as the religion of state is an invitation for value conflicts to be settled according to political power, the manipulation of majority opinion, and the corrosive effect of political correctness on independence of thought, freedom of inquiry, and reasoned debate.
8. If reasoned pathways are ignored or suppressed and liberty slips away, it can only be the citizens that have failed. Such pathways cannot be the responsibility of government or the Constitution. The Constitution takes no position on metaphysics or religion; it was only a piece of the platform of liberty, not the last word.

Human nature, in not being consistently virtuous, requires restraint against evil and inducement toward good that are not dependent on itself. For the cause of freedom, the basis of the restraint and inducement needs to be appealable to reason on all sides—that is, it must be true. The lack of virtue and truth plays into the hands of totalitarian power. The spinelessness of immoderation and moral degeneration is unable to perceive and square up to signs warning of heavy-handed rule; the deception and seduction of high-minded utopian visions prompts too many to buy into the aggression and oppression necessary to achieve them. Ignorance of these points causes our political leaders to sometimes assume that American constitutional liberty can thrive anywhere. It cannot thrive just anywhere, even in America if a basis of voluntary social cohesion that transcends human nature is lost.

CHAPTER 4

TRUTH, THAT WHICH CORRESPONDS TO REALITY[1]

Reason is to the spiritual what eyes are to the physical
—Jay Wilson

Resolutions of controversial and morally charged questions of public interest need to make contact with reality at its root. Otherwise, they will be superficial, and superficial resolutions fall apart sooner or later. The superficial nature of pre-Civil War compromises over slavery was a chief national lesson. We may further ask: Was slavery wrong because the North in the Civil War had a mightier army? Was it wrong because a majority of citizens, North and South, thought it wrong? Or was it objectively wrong independent of what anyone thought? The central question is still the same as that introduced at the beginning of chapter 2: Are right, good, and just determined by power, by individual or majority opinion, or are they fixed external to persons, and if so fixed, how? If externally fixed, *how* is a question the answer to which can be apprehended only by inference, not by perception—whether there is a reality behind the visible reality. Not only are we interested in the validity and truthfulness of propositions on these matters, we are also interested in gaining insight into the ferocity with which they are, at times, insisted upon. One thing should be obvious though: no one is debating the justice of pre-Civil War slavery today. The matter is resolved.

How Belief in a Creator Is (or Is Not) Attained

Here is a question sometimes posed to believers in a creator by non-believers: Are you a presuppositionalist or an evidentialist? Do you presuppose the existence of a creator and then find some evidence to support that, or are you an evidentialist, one who arrives at this answer from a disinterested review of the available evidence? The question may be returned: Is belief in the nonexistence of a creator a presupposition with some evidence clattering along behind, or is it arrived at by a disinterested review? But has anyone ever undertaken a disinterested review? Is it even possible to maintain disinterest in the strict sense of the term *disinterested*? There are, after all, serious ramifications arising from one's answer to the creator question to which no one is immune— the meaning of existence and how one should live, among others. Or does it really matter whether one begins with a presupposition or with evidence if the evidence necessary to confirm one or the other belief is out there to be found?

Though the evidentialist in his or her disinterested review might seem to better satisfy the demands of rationality, evidence does not generate abstract universal theories on its own. Whatever evidence may be gathered from the physical world is pretty remote from the nature of what ends up being concluded—a universal negative as regards the supernatural in one instance, a mind far beyond capabilities with which we are accustomed in another. Evidence must be interpreted, and it is often the case that it may be interpreted in more than one way. Availability of all evidence relevant to such universal conceptions might never be assured. Much more, the gathering of evidence may be selective, and the selection can be decisive. Evidence must be gathered according to some criterion by which it is judged to be relevant or warranted. The most obvious criterion is whether it lends credibility to the answer one is predisposed to accept.

An ambivalence of evidence is not unusual. C.S. Lewis wrote, "What we learn from experience depends on the kind of philosophy we bring to experience."[2] The context of this remark was the relevance of sensory evidence—what is seen, heard, felt—to the miraculous. What might first appear to be miraculous is interpreted according to whether one already believes in such a possibility or not. If not, any evidence may be dismissed as illusion or trickery. Similarly, on such questions as the existence or nonexistence of a creator, one's philosophy or predisposition determines what may be done with any evidence. It should be more honest, therefore, to acknowledge the existence of predispositions than to claim an unprejudiced read of the evidence. The presuppositional versus evidential question is not worthy of further attention.

Arguing over probabilities on this question does not lead anywhere. The appearance of the natural world and universe by the natural processes that science describes is absurdly improbable. In reaction to the astonishingly fine-tuned physical laws necessary for such a universe to exist and the accompanying senseless improbabilities, a perpetually unconfirmable speculation of countless universes in a multiverse is offered. One of them just happens to be habitable. An immaterial creating god seems at least as lofty a speculation as the multiverse theory and a blank begging to be filled in with even more speculations. According to some, the probability of a supernatural event is always less than the least probable of natural events that may explain the existence of something (such as the universe) and, therefore, effectively eliminated. That, however, is just a convenient rule for assuring the preferred answer ahead of time, a philosophy of sorts brought to experience. The world exists despite unfavorable probabilities. One needs to plow other fields than probability to arrive at a natural or supernatural cause.

Is belief in God innate, say, from birth, or is it acquired? If belief is innate, one cannot be argued out of it. Neither can you use your innate belief to convince someone who says they lack it. Innateness might seem to describe the rigidity of humanity over the matter, but people do switch sides. If innate belief is only that God exists and nothing more, it is empty and inconsequential. If innate belief involves more than just *God exists*, it would be impossible to resolve differences that seem invariably to arise in the elaborations of such belief. In my own case, I do not know if there was ever any innate belief; other considerations far surpass and outweigh whatever innate belief there might have been.

The Bible neither states nor implies that belief in God is innate. Neither does it set forth arguments on behalf of the existence of God. In the Bible, the existence of God is flatly presumed. "In the beginning, God created… " is how it begins. This seems to suggest that if you want arguments, you need to figure them out yourself. Most folks are content to pass over that opportunity, perhaps thinking or maybe even hoping that it cannot be done. A seeker of truth should not pass over the opportunity; it is too rich a field.

One argument that will not be advanced here is appeal to nature, for three reasons. First, its wonders notwithstanding, there is an underlying ambiguity about nature. There are certainly many delights and much pleasantness. But there are also tornadoes, hurricanes, earthquakes, floods, volcanoes, tidal waves, blizzards, droughts, famines, plagues, diseases, infirmities, paralyses, and parasites. One is taken, another left. Time after time, when someone expires, nature runs on as if nothing at all has happened—no fairness, no compassion, only indifference. From all that may be inferred from the affidavit of nature, if a creator exists, then that creator is indifferent also, which is equivalent to there being none. Doubtless, there is an argument from nature here that can be appreciated, if not accepted, by most. To some unbelievers, it is inconceivable, if there would be a god, that the objective of creation is not physical perfection. Therefore, because perfection is lacking, there can be no god. A second reason is that it may be a tactical error nowadays to appeal to nature in arguing for the existence of a creator because of the public indoctrination of evolutionary science and its predisposition against creation. Evolutionary science may be sent away by pointing out that the reasoning by which evolutionary science is conducted is not itself scientifically explainable (a pointing out that appears later in this chapter) but that is not an appeal to nature. A third reason to bypass appeal to nature is the unoriginality of conventional wisdom. This is the analogy that says if a mechanical device, such as a watch, has a designer, the far more complex and intricate world of nature must too. That argument has long ago exhausted its promise, though turning it on its head may redeem it somewhat: If design exists in a mechanical device and as we are assured by evolutionary scientists that there is no intelligent design in nature and thus such designs do not arise from nature, then where do they come from? No appeal to nature, therefore; what is found within the mind is more compelling.[3]

The Demand for Coherency

Ventures to gain new knowledge about the world must, at times, assume rationality and order in regions that have not yet been verified by experience to be rational and orderly. Experience does *confirm* that the world is orderly and consistent in its behavior as far as experience can see. Heat from the stove is consistently followed by boiling water in the kettle. As one has seen this pattern recur and expects it to continue in every instance, the boiling water is *always* associated with heat from the stove, anywhere, anytime. Here, the expectation of order and consistency lays the groundwork for positing universal associations of cause and effect from sets of particulars—in this case, a number of instances of heat followed by boiling water to a universal and necessary cause-effect relation between these two conditions. The inductive mode of logic, the move from particulars to universals, is seen to apply as much as experience can verify. However, inferring a universal association does not *assure* the reality of a universal association. The mind "reads" a universal rationality into the world; it is not gained from experience.

Science thrives, in fact, *depends* on the idea that a consistent rationality orders the universe. The laws of nature are posed as applying at all times and places, even though experience can never verify that. Thus, the universal lawful ordering of nature is an assumption. But with that assumption in hand, scientists proceed to infer much knowledge about that world that cannot be experienced directly. They posit laws governing planetary motion, the nature of gravity, various types of subatomic particles, nuclear forces, dark matter, and dark energy. They even go so far as to make quite remarkable claims about the natural world that are contrary to intuition and accepted wisdom. In Einsteinian physics, for example, time and space are not absolute and invariant dimensions; only the speed of light is invariant. The reason scientists can do that is because they assume the natural world to be rational and consistent with the utmost strictness. Einstein proceeded to devise his successful theory of general relativity on the philosophical ground of utmost rigor in the consistency between the laws of mechanical motion and the laws of electromagnetism. His "experiments" in relativity theory were really only mental constructs, experiments conducted in his mind. Einstein did not arrive at his astonishing conclusions by observing the physical world. Yet the empirical validity of the theory has since been verified. Although the idea has not always been present, in Western civilization since the scientific revolution at least, everyone is accustomed to regarding the natural world as one that is thoroughly and consistently rational, even to the point of conforming to the rigorous logic of mathematical formulas.

But the idea has theological foundations. Scientists assume the universe to be ordered according to such an extreme of rationality because at the time that scientific methods were being devised during the sixteenth and seventeenth centuries, the most successful scientists believed in a rational creator. Copernicus, Kepler, Galileo, and Newton believed that the natural world was rational because the Creator was rational. That the natural world was rationally ordered and discoverable by rational inquiry was, in fact, a deduction from an understanding of the Creator as a rational creator. That was the thinking of Nicolaus Copernicus (1473–1543) when, in contradistinction to nearly the entire history of thinking on the subject, he positioned the sun at the center of the known universe instead of the Earth. Copernicus could not square the arbitrary complexity of the second century Ptolemaic mathematical model of the Earth-centered universe with a supremely rational and orderly creator. The mathematics of heliocentrism was superior in its simplicity, and he knew it was correct on that basis. Even though it took much time before enough evidence and theoretical understanding—principally from Kepler, Galileo, and Newton—came together to convince everyone about the sun's centrality, the supporting evidence and theoretical insight did arrive. Copernicus's idea about the sun and the planets eventually proved itself more than a mathematical contrivance.

Scientific rationality did not just pop into existence; it was queued up by the spirit of the prior age. A serious problem for many in the academic world is that the prior age was supposed to have been the age when the heavy cloud of religious ignorance darkened the expansive potential of the mind—the Dark Ages. It was supposed to have been the age of regression, superstition, and intellectual imprisonment. So how was the supposed Dark Age, the age during which the academic world's own foundations were set, the very idea of the university, the *universitas magistrorum et scholarium*? The University of Paris was founded at about 1150, Oxford in 1167, and Cambridge in 1209. Twenty-four more universities were founded in Europe before the end of the fourteenth century and at least twenty-eight more before the end of the fifteenth.[4]

Religion and rationality had never before been so tightly intertwined as in the medieval universities. The encounter between twelfth century Catholicism and ancient Greek philosophical writings became Greek-inspired rationality applied to religious understanding— the study of theology. The *Summa Theologiae* of Thomas Aquinas (1224 or 1225–74), appearing in separate volumes between 1265 and 1274, became the pinnacle of the era's theological output. Rational argument informed theology and supplemented divine revelation. In this, religion was neither invalidated nor diminished. Indeed, the subjection of medieval Christianity to rational analysis only clarified an understanding of the Creator as a rational creator. Equally remarkable was the autonomy to pursue such analysis of religion in the first place. Not every religion would be comfortable with that.

It has been often claimed that in the medieval era, China and the Islamic empire owned more mathematical prowess, intellectual wherewithal, and technological know-how than did Western Europe. Why, then, did these cultures not produce a scientific program? Why did the China of the Middle Ages with its technological innovation and independently developed mathematics not begin a scientific program? Why did the mathematicians and astronomers of the Islamic empire with their access to Greek philosophical treatises not sustain continuing progress in those fields? Even more, ancient Greece seems to have had the necessary intellectual, philosophical, and possibly even empirical foundations. Why did a scientific program not arise there? The reason these cultures did not generate a scientific program as it arose in Western Europe is because their views of reality did not suggest that such a program would be profitable. In all three cases, whatever the universe consisted of, it was not the work of a rational creator. Either the natural world was uncreated, eternal, and mystical, or they imagined meddling gods who work by caprice and fiat, not by rational order and principle. These were their religious beliefs. No other view of reality than that of a rational creator was able to suggest that how the universe is organized and run could be rationally figured out. The scientific revolution was inspired by belief in a rational universe handed to it by medieval Christian theology—a theology that was itself a thoroughly rational enterprise.[5] Science did not triumph by shoving religion out of the way as many historians and academics insist. Nothing is gained by continuing to feign puzzlement as to why a scientific program emerged when and where it did.

Over and over again, scientists repeat a characteristic pattern of thought: the assumption of universal rationality leading to inferences about general principles that rule the natural world leading to the quest for empirical confirmation of those principles by observation or experimentation. Whenever an inference or hypothesis has been repeatedly confirmed, scientists assert to have discovered a coherency, typically presented as a scientific theory or possibly even a universal law of nature.[6] Later on in its history, once the extreme rationality of nature was securely in orbit, science was able to jettison its theological booster stage. Accordingly, in subsequent centuries, many scientists as well as philosophers went on to express doubt about the existence of any creator in the first place. That there was any metaphysical reality at all was held in question, even contempt in scientific circles. Their thinking was that the laws governing natural processes were sufficient to produce all the effects seen in nature, tacitly including their own minds in that. In leaving behind the earlier fortuitous correlation between theology and natural philosophy, an atheistic trend of thought emerged, extremely skeptical toward the supernatural.

Nevertheless, consistency and rationality are first a demand and only second a discovery. Science assumes and, heaven forbid, has faith that there is a coherency in nature, and science's theories are, in part, the product of that faith. In fact, sometimes in the earnestness to discover the coherency, orderings have been imposed on nature that do not truly describe it. Theories may be wrong, and many theories initially thought to have been sound have been found in error later on and either corrected or replaced. Theories such as the geocentric universe, circular planetary orbits, the ether theory of light propagation, and a static, non-expanding universe have been found in error. Newtonian gravitation has been found to be of limited applicability. The instances of erroneous theories or theories of limited applicability demonstrate that demand precedes discovery—discovery, that is, of the truer order in nature. It is almost as if the absence of coherency is intolerable. But certainly, the desire for truer and more comprehensive understanding drives continued scientific inquiry into further undiscovered coherencies that may yet be present in nature.

It might have been the case that nature exhibited nothing of the sought-after coherency. Suppose all hypotheses to this point had failed. What then? Should we have given up the quest? Perhaps we would still think in terms of ends to be achieved and means to achieve them—at least manipulating environments more to our liking would not have ceased. Yet to think in means-ends terms, it is necessary to assume some cause-effect rationality that desired ends will be achieved by means under consideration at least in one's immediate circumstances. If cause-effect rationality was to be given up, means-ends thinking would have to be given up along with it. But no, means-ends thinking shall not be given up. The quest and the demand for cause-effect rationality precede its discovery. *Rationality exists whether nature exhibits it or not.* And if there would ever again be a need to secure the validity of rational inference into the composition and operation of the natural world beyond a mere assumption or expectation, it would need to be by means of theology. That at least is how the early scientists secured it.

Uncomfortable Incongruities

The Value of Survival

There is an assortment of uncomfortable incongruities in which an exclusively scientific view of reality finds itself enmeshed. One of these is that a conglomeration of molecules should try to survive as a conglomeration—in particular, those conglomerations known as living things. Among the findings of evolutionary science is that living things have often gained survival advantages as a consequence of escalating complexity. Thus, it may be certain that the more advanced the form of life on the evolutionary tree, the more finely tuned and successful have been its adaptations for survival. But the question about the mechanisms of survival—the particulars of evolutionary theory involving random mutation and natural selection—does not answer the question as to the *why* of survival. Why should it be a matter of concern that a conglomeration of molecules remains intact? Why should anything try to survive? What is gained by such survival? These questions are not within the scope of scientific inquiry, but they should be if science presumes to explain living things. No one can deny the legitimacy of such questions without nullifying the value of their own survival.

There is no question that human beings want to survive. The desire to survive may not often rise above a subconscious level. But without survival intent, one might just as readily adopt behavior that causes death and dispersal as that which permits continued living. It would not matter. But it does matter. Persons act in ways to assure their own survival, and living, they say, is good, or at least should be. Even those who terminate their lives intentionally do not often do so on a whim; there is typically a regrettable history of distress leading up to the decision. To discern the value of survival, one has only to consider laws against murder in their universal appeal to something of higher value than conglomerations of molecules or observe how heroic are efforts to maintain the survival of someone hanging on its edge.

How, then, do you get from adaptations advantageous to survival to value placed on survival? Material objects, including living things, do not have an inherent value that can be discerned by studying them. The value of anything, including survival, is not discovered by empirical inquiry but rather assigned. As value is assigned, it is not a productive avenue of scientific inquiry. The holding of value is something associated with the holder rather than the object. So while a scientific theory may speculate as to causes of the *fact* of survival, it cannot license a finding about the *value* of survival. But from the phraseology used such as the "struggle for survival" and "survival of the fittest" (if *fittest* is a judgment of value), it would seem that evolutionary theory is saturated with the value of survival. Is the value of survival subsumed or implicit within the theory or not? If the value of survival is denied, then it is a denial of what is known and claimed, even if known and claimed subjectively. If the value of survival is admitted, it cannot, in principle, be accounted for scientifically. Neither position is sustainable.

The Value of Truth

A second incongruity to ponder is why Galileo (1564–1642) kept insisting that the Earth is not the center of the universe when that insistence did not enhance his prospects for survival. There are, no doubt, legitimate questions about the propriety of the Roman Catholic Church's methods of persuasion in Galileo's case. But aside from those questions, as intelligent as Galileo was, one would expect that he had figured out that survival was the real game, even before Charles Darwin (1809–82) had named it. Galileo did end up favoring survival. To a point though, his motivation was truth about the configuration of the universe, not survival. In fact, both parties in the conflict about the configuration of the universe viewed the true answer as having value. There is such a thing as the value of truth, and scientists may often be found vigorously defending scientific theories as if whether or not they stand as true is worth their trouble. This is especially the case with evolutionary theory but which, considering its exclusively scientific formulation and in the interest of scientific self-consistency of sticking to facts, ought rather to have no value attached to it at all.

We have now two motivating factors in human behavior: the value truth and the value of survival. As in Galileo's case, there exist situations where they may be in conflict. Unfortunately, the fact that there are such conflicts adds no credibility to the idea that natural selection, which operates on a survival criterion, has somehow produced a creature also skilled in matters of truth, in addition to survival. You cannot posit a process in which the criterion for success is truth as arising out of a process in which the criterion for success is survival. We will have to wait and see what scientists drum up to explain how truth is congruent with survival. We may be waiting a long time. The possibility of truth in evolutionary science, for example, is not dependent on the survival of evolutionary science. It could still contain truth even if forgotten. It may continue to survive even if untrue. Truth and survival are not aligned by some universal necessity. If evolutionary scientists would ever attempt to account for scientific truth, they would have to account for it as an effect of a natural selection process in which the criterion for success is survival—no matter how many steps are inserted in between. But the attainment of scientific truth is really a quite different object than survival. Ask Galileo!

If science deals with matters of fact and not value, accounts of these factors—the value of survival and the value of truth—cannot be delivered by science. If the presence or absence of a cause, say, a biological process, determines the presence or absence of a holding of value, it is a question of fact. The question of whether there really is value in whatever it is that is held or not held valuable remains open. The value that scientists hold toward their own enterprise would seem to be scientifically inexplicable.

The Distinctiveness of Rational Inference

Scientific insight into the composition and operation of the natural world is attained by rational inference. By rational inference, science is able to ascertain vast knowledge about the universe that cannot be observed directly—such knowledge, for example, as laws governing planetary motion, the nature of gravity, and the existence of various subatomic particles, nuclear forces, dark matter, and dark energy as mentioned already. Inferences may take an explanatory form, giving account of observed effects in terms of hypothesized causes outside the reach of observation. Or inferences may be predictive, positing future effects from causes now under study.

But to infer the cause of an event or phenomenon, or to explain and predict an effect, is a process distinct from the cause-effect operation itself. Inferences are ventures to gain knowledge beyond the reach of experience, are always about something other than themselves, may be true or false, and are deliberative, never inevitable. A cause-effect process, on the other hand, proceeds inevitably, is never about something, and produces no knowledge. To consider effects as true or false is absurd. No doubt, scientific knowledge depends on the validity of causation. How else to hypothesize about causes beyond the reach of experience or about effects not yet observed? Without the validity of causation, science would be unable to acquire knowledge of anything beyond sensory experience. But what nature does and what may be inferred about it are two different things.[7]

Following the boiling water example above, consider scientific insight into the cause-effect relations governing steam cycles. Same as any other scientific hypotheses, there was once a venture to gain knowledge of physical principles. Then began the science of thermodynamics—specifically how energy is transferred from heat into mechanical force and the thermal properties of H2O. The four laws of thermodynamics were discovered. But such knowledge was not among the effects of water being converted into steam or condensed back again. Water, heat, and the potential for consequent useful motion have been in existence longer than the science of thermodynamics, which arrived only in the mid-nineteenth century. Cause-effect processes of nature may produce all manner of effects, but the knowledge of those processes is not one of them.

Here, science is on firm ground; it can take rationality for granted. It does not need to account for the inferring mind; it just applies it. Evolutionary science, though, is in trouble. It is in trouble because of the implicit claim to have accounted for the inferring mind. If it ever ventures to offer an account of rational inference, it would have to do so, as already noted, in terms of natural selection—a rational creature mutated from an instinctive creature and natural selection then favored the rational creature. In this, rationality would have its basis in cause and effect, if not outright chance. But as knowledge of anything beyond experience is not caused but inferred, an account of rational inference as arising from causation adds nothing. Such an account would itself be an inference about an occurrence beyond experience. Thus, the validity of rational inference must already be assured prior to drawing such an inference and assured on some other platform.

To put all this as straightforwardly as possible, you cannot climb out of the world of cause and effect with scientific knowledge in hand except by having brought rational inference with you on the way in. Real progress in understanding the coherencies and orderings of the universe is being achieved. But there is more required in the practice of science than what the evolutionary construct accommodates. What the evolutionary theorists need to show, and either do not or cannot, is how rationality emerged out of a biological cause-effect process. We advance the proposition then that scientific reasoning is not a natural process.

Scientific Imperialism

Because of its metaphysical ramifications, evolutionary science attracts wider interest than just among scientists. Non-scientists are also found engaged in vigorous defense as well as opposition. The wider participation was seen in debates between evolutionary science advocates and advocates of creation science and intelligent design in the associated court cases of past decades. Clearly, evolutionary science stirs up interest outside of scientific circles because there are non-scientific interests and agendas riding on the success of the theories that many seek to advance or oppose. It is, therefore, necessary to distinguish between science and evolutionary science and to consider more precisely what lurks beneath the mere fact of the wider interest.

No doubt, the wider interest is found in the fact that the metaphysical ramifications are far-reaching and profound. In particular, the metaphysical reach of the Bible and Christianity not only subordinates all physical existence but also extends into conscience— not particularly pleasant to those who have no interest in moral accountability to anyone outside of themselves. Though evolutionary science presumes to nullify that reach, something more is thought necessary. The best defense is a good offense, and so the response of the anti-metaphysicians and secularists seems to be for science to explain away religion in scientific terms. Yes, religion must be analyzed as an evolutionary adaptation of sorts. (For that matter, maybe science should too.) But as much as science reduces religion to an evolutionary phenomenon that may be studied scientifically, science is still pretty useless for figuring out what is right and good. When justice is violated or when truth is violated, explanations are demanded... but not from science. The scientific analysis of religion and scientific theories as to its origin are the latest example of over-the-top scientific imperialism.

Objecting to Everyone Else's Objections

There is no point in continuing to beat a dead horse as the saying goes. But for the purpose of education in the realm of ideas, we will do a little of that anyway. The horse in question is an intellectual trend residing under the umbrella of postmodernism. The horse died when a paper written by physicist Alan Sokal, "Transgressing the Boundaries: Towards a Transformative Hermeneutics of Quantum Gravity," presuming to critique quantum gravity theory, appeared in the postmodern journal *Social Text* in 1996. The "critique" had only the appearance of a critique; it was actually a hoax. The paper consisted of a heavy dose of postmodern rhetoric—postmodern literary candy not intended to make any sense—with a view to the end of being licked up by the trendy journal's editors. Following on the heels of an assortment of other postmodern trends by the late twentieth century, it had become fashionable in the humanities sector of academia to question the objectivity of science. Scientific theories were purported to be merely the constructions and power gaming of a certain domineering social group, hard-science scientists.

Baiting the journal's editors along the lines of this trend, the paper pretended that quantum gravity theory was a constructed ideological tool with a social agenda rather than a legitimate scientific theory.

The project was successful; the editors of *Social Text* swallowed the article whole. The hoax made known the duplicity and hypocrisy of postmodern academics—the fact that they, in their intellectual arrogance, failed to exercise enough rigor to recognize the hoax. Sokal quickly announced the "uncontrolled" experiment in a different academic journal, *Lingua Franca*. The experiment was necessary, he later explained, because postmodern academic literature had gone too far in its attacks on the objectivity of science. This was, he said, not so much to the detriment of science but to the detriment of the progressive political agenda (of which he is a proponent) because it was diverting leftist intellectual talents into useless pursuits.[8]

Though science does have philosophical entanglements and undercurrents where it departs from empirical verifiability, the essential objectivity of science's methods is sound and worthy of cultural deference… on scientific questions. Science works and works exceedingly well. Nevertheless, despite the ridiculousness of postmodern academic literature, of which Sokal's experiment was a worthy parody, and though dead it may be, the appeal of postmodern thinking has already long infiltrated the culture. It is worthwhile, therefore, to take a high-level look at postmodern thought, if only to show for posterity its sinister character. This is especially the case where postmodern tactics have been applied against forms of transcendence.

The horse driving the postmodern bandwagon is a delight in setting up a sort of "super-philosophy" where judgment is cast on everyone else's philosophy as having only local, not universal applicability. The postmodern denial of universal meta-narratives, meta-narratives being what philosophies or metaphysical positions are called, was an attempt to eliminate the coercion of a single absolutized truth such as science or Marxism or Christianity or Islam.[9] Yet in this endeavor, postmodernism became a universal meta-narrative itself, belittling all others as non-universal. Thus, there are no universally true propositions. The postmodern view is that there are no vantage points from which to view ultimate reality. There are only invented "truths," each powering to achieve social and political supremacy. All is subjective, except, of course, postmodernism itself. In essence, postmodern discourse attempts to tear down anything exhibiting coherence, meaning, originality, or authenticity. Any traditionally recognized textual authority such as the Bible or the Constitution is to be regarded as propaganda in service to a social-political power agenda.

The application of postmodern critical methodology, as far as it concerns us here, is that the instant that any argument is advanced in support of the existence of a transcendent reality, such as a creator, it is subcategorized as a religious argument. This means, according to postmodern thinking, that it is a "truth" applicable only within that particular religious context. Neither the argument nor its conclusion has any standing or meaning outside its group of adherents. Under the administration of postmodernism, there is "your truth" and there is "my truth" but there is no "the truth." Therefore, the "truth" that you find most convenient is the "truth" you may want to adopt and follow. That is good postmodern advice. "We maintain that dogmas of a religious nature are neither true nor false but are among many alternative stories in terms of which the world may be understood," they say. Whoa, Horsey! What is one supposed to do with that?

The postmodern onslaught against the possibility of an objective metaphysical reality appears formidable. But it is a dead horse. A first indication is found in the denunciatory nature of postmodernism itself. A postmodernist deems those who regard their view of matters involving metaphysics, or involving values and morality, as universally true as having a problem. Their problem, according to the postmodernist, is in thinking that their own platform is universally applicable and that other views are less true or even false. No one is authorized to object to anything outside their own localized sphere of belief. But in objecting to everyone else's objections, postmodernists have their own objection. This is hypocrisy.

A second indication is found in logic. The law of noncontradiction is the most fundamental of the laws of logic.[10] In one form, it says that a proposition cannot both be true and self-contradictory. In another, it says that two contradictory propositions cannot both be true. We see at once that the idea of truth is built into logic. Now it may well be the case that many noncontradictory propositions are not self-evidently true, but at least there is no law of logic that would hang the statement "Truth exists." Where truth becomes a quest, contradictions cannot remain.

Of course, now we are supposed to accept a soup of cultural diversity wherein contradictory metaphysical positions bubble up from time to time and coexist adjacent to each other in some kind of harmony. All this is supposed to happen without anyone ever objecting to anything. But can a mind be content with contradictions? A culture may remain contradictory and incoherent, but an individual mind self-destructs on that drug. Does a mind not have something to say? You cannot argue against the need for coherence and expect to escape being incoherent. An individual is supposed to be indivisible—that is the root of the term. But fragmentation and contradiction are what postmodernism is all about.[11] It claims for itself status as a universal meta-narrative, which claim cannot be true according to its own assertion that there are no universally true propositions. In addition to being hypocrites, then, in their own universal assertions about reality that nothing is universal and true, they must also be liars. Do not be deceived; postmodernism is itself only an invented "truth" powering to achieve supremacy.

The Western mind once learned to demand that the law of noncontradiction apply to the world, even when initial indications seemed to suggest that the world *was* contradictory, mystical and capricious, enchanted, and haunted by spirits. The enterprise of science is arguably the best example of this unquenchable sense of a rational world. Science must assume the validity of objective truth in nature in order to even begin its investigations. Science cannot afford to indulge in incoherence. But if science demands rationality and coherency in nature *and gets it*, why should the same not be demanded of the metaphysical? If scientists draw inferences about objects and properties of the universe that cannot be observed directly, why should inferences not be drawn about what else cannot be observed directly?

The Complexity of Minds

Ontology is the branch of philosophy that deals with the nature of being or existence.[12] It attempts to answer the question "What exists?" The question is most particularly directed toward what may exist beyond the reach of sensory perception and experience. A negative answer simplifies the ontological landscape considerably. The simplification in practical terms is this: If there is no god, then there is no need to worry about complicating expectations that might be imposed on anyone by such god. Everyone should be permitted to do whatever they please, free from disapproval, as long as, say, everyone plays fair and there is no harm to others.

But a negative answer is *too* simple. There *are* complicating expectations. Even the minimal expectations of fair play and no harm often go unsatisfied. There is a tension. What one ought to do is not always the same as what one does. What one ought not to do and what one does not do are often two different things. There are imperatives on behavior that are distinguishable from actual behavior. As everyone well knows, even laws and associated penalties fail to align behavior with such oughts and ought nots. C.S. Lewis points out in Book One of *Mere Christianity*, the book titled "Right and Wrong as a Clue to the Meaning of the Universe," how this distinction between desired and actual behavior radically alters what may be concluded about the nature of the universe.[13] There is a shared sense of right, good, and just that everyone appeals to in their moral pronouncements but that no one is quite able to modify to their advantage. High ideals coexist with lower attractions and people get tangled up crosswise by their lower selves in oughts and ought nots, even as they try to tie up others in the same cords.[14]

It is typical to want to appear as if one is in alignment with moral imperatives, even though one might not be. The pragmatic mind rules, calculating what behavior and speech should be advantageous for appearances at the moment. It is noteworthy that an inquiry into the first documented crime was immediately hit by an obstacle thrown up for the purpose of maintaining an appearance of innocence. "Where is Abel, your brother?" "I do not know. Am I my brother's keeper?"[15]

It is also widely hoped and believed that social conventions exhaust the possibilities as to what defines the moral landscape. The expectations of fair play and no harm originate only from the general will of village, town, city, state, region, or country. If there should be any other expectations, they certainly cannot originate external to these whereabouts. The specifics of social conventions (or social contracts) are flexible, varying from time to time and from place to place. Morality and ethics as social convention permits the sense of good and evil to be eased up if it should become intolerably rigid in the excessive application by some. An over-active conscience may be put at rest while still leaving enough rigidity on some other point to beat down others. It is only necessary to set just one small, added prohibition: that against the possibility of unwelcome commandments, which, by pretense of some, are presumed to have dropped down from on high. No need to load up folks with heavy burdens.

Thus, many are delighted to see the Ten Commandments stricken from public view. Their absolutist, prohibitionary, dictatorial tone is unacceptably narrow-minded, unyielding, and intolerant. But they may be too hasty in their denunciation. If the commandments were rewritten from a different point of view, they might want to get them hung back up and the more quickly. That is, if they were inverted—*your life is inviolable, your trust is inviolable, your property is inviolable, your name and reputation are inviolable*—perhaps then, how the second table of the Ten Commandments doubles as unalienable rights might become more apparent. Maybe they might also realize that the manner in which they apply their own "Thou shall not utter narrow-minded, bigoted, intolerant opinions" commandment is as absolute and unyielding as anything that might have dropped down from on high.

A confrontation described in Luke chapter 13 highlights the intuitive, seemingly innate and resilient nature of the sense of good and evil. The Lord Jesus had healed a woman in a synagogue who had been bent over with an infirmity. It happened to be the Sabbath, a day on which, according to religious tradition, only such activities as were expressly authorized were permissible.

> But the ruler of the synagogue, indignant because Jesus had healed on the sabbath, said to the people, "There are six days on which work ought to be done; come on those days and be healed, and not on the sabbath day." Then the Lord answered him, "You hypocrites! Does not each of you on the sabbath untie his ox or his ass from the manger, and lead it away to water it? And ought not this woman, a daughter of Abraham, whom Satan has bound for eighteen years be loosed from this bond on the sabbath day?" As he said this, his adversaries were put to shame; and all the people rejoiced at all the glorious things that were done by him.[16]

Here, the sense of good and evil was not overtaken by convention, custom, or tradition. A tradition of what was permissible to do on the Sabbath that excluded anything not explicitly included could not withstand an occurrence that everyone recognized as goodness. Goodness as social convention does not fare well here. There is something that resists such top down adaptations of justice. There is something that puts restraint on what might otherwise be adaptability to social convention. People know what is right and good; you can see that in what gets played up in eulogies. You can see it also in the examples of Peter and Judas, conscience-stricken after having betrayed a trust.[17] What hinders attempts to reformulate or reinvent the right, good, and just? Whatever the answer, goodness that drifts or that can be modified is not true goodness and will surely give way before any appeal on some point of controversy that reaches out to it. Events in day-to-day living and the crime report on the five o'clock news further serve to keep the reality of absolute good and absolute evil roaring back repeatedly.

The prerequisites for such a thing as conscience to exist are these: (1) awareness of moral coordinates that one cannot alter and does not entirely keep and (2) autonomy from cause and effect that introduces the prospect of moral dilemmas, of choosing between alternative actions that have differing moral implications. Take either of these away, and conscience could not exist. Without the coordinates there would be no distinction between right and wrong or between good and evil, and if the imperatives to do right and good were always kept, there would be no awareness of an internal conflict between moral imperatives and past behavior. Without autonomy, responsibility for choosing properly is an empty concept.

Scientific naturalism is unable to offer explanatory insight into these prerequisites. All one has to do is to note what sort of explanations *are* demanded to account for morally regrettable states of affairs. Scientific explanations, either in terms of natural selection or some other cause-effect process, whether at the biochemical level, the sociological level, or anything in between, are seldom, if ever, accepted. The sorts of explanations that are accepted are those that assume personal responsibility. Personal responsibility hinges on the presence of rationality and autonomy or free will—that someone *ought* to have understood the morally proper course of action and *ought* to have chosen accordingly. Unsatisfied oughts and ought nots cannot be passed off as evolutionary adaptations advantageous for survival. There is more to reality than what scientific methods and theories can grasp.

Crossroads of decision repeatedly confront persons in their awareness of the coordinates of good and evil. But mere awareness of good and evil does not provide sufficient power to bring about right outcomes consistently, especially as that awareness tends to kick in only *after* a wrong turn. Thoughts become very complex as the mind attempts to function within a bind between awareness of behavioral expectations that it cannot determine or control and past behavior that has failed to square up. By reasonings, justifications, and deceptions, it attempts to justify to the outside world, and to itself, a cover of good intentions, or else by concocting false appearances or by secrecy, attempts to conceal behavior. The bind, however, cannot truly be relieved by reasoning or concealment. Knowledge of coordinates is too acute; it is applied against others continually. Awareness of transgression is the cause of many troubles as persons seek to escape the internal accusatory finger of their conscience. One is locked into a condition from which one cannot escape—a condition that has never been more completely explained than by the tree of the knowledge of good and evil in Genesis chapter 3 and its after effects. Freedom is sought by attacking the system, by forming delusions that deny the invariance and universality of rightness, goodness, and justice, or by denying metaphysical reality altogether. The prophet Jeremiah was familiar with the phenomenon: "The heart is deceitful above all things, and desperately corrupt; who can understand it?"[18] It was because of such complexity that John the Baptist was sent to "make straight the way of the Lord."[19]

A negative answer to the question of whether there is a metaphysical reality is too simple. Conscience and the associated complexity of minds cannot be explained without a more elaborate ontology. While knowledge of God is not innate, the knowledge of good and evil is, and the knowledge of God is only one step away from the knowledge of good and evil.[20]

If Anyone Has Ears to Hear, Let Him Hear[21]

The first ontological complication introduced by a positive answer to the question of whether there is a god is "Which god?" It is quite true that there has never been a time in history during which there was a shortage of ideas about gods. Ask any atheist or secularist. Certainly, the oddest, though possibly also the shrewdest answer ever advanced against the apparent confusion of "Which god?" was a god who identified himself as I AM WHO I AM. That was the name of the God of Abraham, the God of Isaac, and the God of Jacob as declared to Moses at the burning bush on Mount Horeb after Moses had asked, "If I come to the people of Israel and say to them, 'The God of your fathers has sent me to you,' and they ask me, 'What is his name?' what shall I say to them?"[22]

The reality of I AM WHO I AM was not a question or matter of debate among the Jews during Old Testament times. The I AM WHO I AM was who He was and remained who He was throughout the thousand-year span of Old Testament writings irrespective of whatever ideas anyone ventured to advance about gods that might be out there. The Old Testament tells how the Jews were themselves repeatedly and sorely yanked back to consciousness of that reality—a reality away from which they would sharply veer anytime the voice of that reality, the I AM's spokesmen (the prophets), was not pressing upon them. "They have turned aside quickly out of the way which I commanded them"[23] begins a theme running throughout the Old Testament. From Isaiah chapter 1 to Malachi chapter 4, the prophets run a near-continuous discourse of hot displeasure toward the I AM's people, repeatedly threatening them with disaster and extinction because of their failure to adhere to the commandments. When one prophet asked how long he should continue with such prophesying, the answer came back, "Until cities lie waste without inhabitant, and houses without men, and the land is utterly desolate."[24] What god invented by a people would so continually contend with them against their inclinations?

Against the inclinations of the people toward manufactured idolatry, for example, there was no shortage of condemnations in the Old Testament. Lest someone think that the prophets made the whole thing up and were scheming to gain advantage from the people's susceptibility to supernatural beliefs, they were uniformly the targets of the people's irritation and resentment. Glimpses of the opposition and hostility in the book of Jeremiah should eliminate doubt about this point.[25] The occupation of prophet did not seem terribly high on the list of sought-after careers. But it was the records of these writing prophets, as reproof and warning-heavy as they were, that the scribes meticulously maintained over the centuries. Though there were plenty of other prophets with more favorable messages,[26] only these messages were preserved. What further distinguishes the writing prophets, and perhaps is the reason for the preservation of their work, is the forward-looking character: Interspersed among the words of woe are references to the restoration of Israel as an independent kingdom and deliverance from their enemies.[27] But after famines, invasions, deportations, and enemies round about, the Old Testament ends with no such restoration or deliverance in sight.

The Old Testament is not the end of the book; there is a New Testament invariably attached to it. Some 400 years after Judaism's last prophet penned the final words of the last book of the Old Testament, along came the New Testament. This appendage, however, was written by purveyors of Christianity, not by preservers of Judaism. Christianity was soon recognized as a distinct religion, not a sect of Judaism; it was decided early on that Gentile converts to Christianity did not first need to convert to Judaism.[28] At that point, the Old Testament might have shaken off this upstart and Christianity escaped from weary laws. But as distant in the past and as geographically remote as the appearing of a man claiming to be the king and deliverer of a tribe of Middle Easterners now is, the ground on which that appearance may continue to be taken seriously is the Old Testament anticipation. In this, the Old Testament is seen to function as a template of sorts, qualifying later events that happen to conform to its predictions. Indeed, in hindsight it is clear that conformance to the Old Testament is the certificate of authenticity for whatever subsequent religious developments could and would be joined to it.[29] It was just that the restoration and deliverance ended up being of a form unanticipated by anyone—try resurrection.

The apostle Paul wrote plainly that the death, burial, and resurrection of the Lord Jesus was "according to the scriptures."[30] At the time he wrote that, the scriptures consisted exclusively of the Old Testament writings. Whenever he came to a new place in his travels as an apostle (or missionary), he customarily reasoned "from the scriptures, explaining and proving that it was necessary for the Christ to suffer and to rise from the dead, saying, 'This Jesus, who I proclaim to you, is the Christ.'"[31] The first several verses of Acts chapter 17 describe Paul's first visit to the city of Thessalonica. Later on, he wrote letters to the church he had established there: the first and second letters of Paul to the Thessalonians. But 1 and 2 Thessalonians are among the first New Testament books written. The Old Testament scriptures are the scriptures he reasoned from on his first visit there and every other place he visited. These were places where those scriptures were being read every Sabbath in the synagogues[32] and people were familiar with them. The references to their contents were decisive in substantiating the message being announced by Paul. (See also Appendix C: To What May Be Attributed the Increase and Expansion of Christianity?)

Amid ever present confusion and diversity in the realm of the metaphysical, the message of Christianity came into the world unexpectedly as a reasoned appeal. The message was resisted by most of those to whom it was first delivered, the Jews. Jewish leaders vigorously opposed it, fearing the loss of their station. First, they, then later, Roman governing authorities, exerted coercive pressure, threats, and violence against acceptance. The message was a threat to their regulation of religion. But these tactics failed to overcome reasoned persuasion. The appeals to the Old Testament writings stood fast. Whatever coercive tactics and machinations have been applied on behalf of Christianity in the centuries following Constantine, they are irrelevant to its origination.

Surpassing and outweighing abstract philosophical arguments for the existence of God, the veracity of the appeal that the Bible *is* the word of God remains fixed on two principal assurances:

1. The foundations of Christianity were written into the Old Testament long before Christianity ever appeared— conclusive evidence of the existence of one plan and one mind behind that plan.
2. Christianity was established largely on the authority of the Old Testament in the face of Jewish rejection and opposition— conclusive evidence that the Old Testament was not a Jewish invention.

Although Jewish leaders were hostile to Christianity, the Old Testament's conceptual patterns and images are not. If there is a plan embedded in the Old Testament and it was not a plan devised by Jews, then whose plan is it? One may question the reports of miracles, but it must be admitted that the nature of the New Testament miracles is entirely consistent with the message of eternal life being communicated—the blind see, the lame walk, lepers are cleansed, the deaf hear, and the dead are raised.[33] It should not be thought uncritical to believe that miracles would accompany a supernatural intrusion, if there should be such a thing. Indeed, a supernatural intrusion would be insufficiently demonstrated without them. But it may be more the everyday miracle that establishes the credibility of miracles— the mind that, quite apart from causation, demands evidence before believing them.

Concluding Remarks

Not to make too much of it, but it was the father of modern philosophy, Rene Descartes, who wrote *Cogito ergo sum* (I think; therefore, I am). Consciousness of thought—the mind—is the first known reality. The reality of the mind is affirmed even in the doubting of its existence. This was Descartes's foundation for defeating the skepticism to which all empirical methods of inquiry are vulnerable. The most radical such skepticism posits the possibility of a deceitful supernatural entity, an evil genius in Descartes's words that feeds your senses so as to make you believe in a material world that may not, in fact, exist. The defeat of such skepticism is made possible by the mind not being in essence a thing to be perceived; no sensory perception is necessary to know that one's mind exists. It is a non-material, non-physical consciousness that is open to rationality. That realization does not get you confirmation of a material world, but the material world would seem, nevertheless, to be the medium through which minds may convey rationality to one another.

There is a necessary corollary: Non-material consciousness and rationality, if they exist, cannot be derived from material things or from what may be observed or perceived. Evolutionary constructs of the unobserved past are self-defeating because they make the mind a byproduct of the material world and biology. That self-defeat steps out into plain view as one considers that the evolutionary constructs themselves have to be admitted as further byproducts of the same biology. After that, there is no thought that would not likewise exist as a byproduct. And there is nothing left to establish the superiority of an evolutionary construct above any non-evolutionary construct; both would equally be the effects of biological causation. Whatever causation produces exists. Whether such constructs are true or false is irrelevant to causation. Causation is not, of course, how the mind operates. Evolutionary constructs are themselves an outcome of reasoning—reasoning by which one is able to attempt to justify such constructs. It is just that you cannot draw reasoning out of causation.

Tiring of contradictions, incoherence, hypocrisy, and irrelevance, there is another super-philosophy to which one may turn. It stands quietly in opposition to the postmodern super-philosophy. There is, however, a cost to enter. It is necessary to leave behind contempt for any truth that does not proceed from one's self—the self as final reality. It is necessary to drop all pretenses to playing God.

CHAPTER 5

Freedom in a Godless World

Justice is turned back, and righteousness stands afar off; for truth has fallen in the public squares, and uprightness cannot enter. Truth is lacking, and he who departs from evil makes himself a prey.

—Isaiah 59:14–15, RSV

A View of Freedom

The *seven* paragraphs that follow illustrate the style of argument that tends to be advanced in defense of a secular or humanistic freedom—moral relativism generally, freedom from certain moral restraints more specifically. The secular/humanistic worldview now dominates Western civilization, and it is worth noting that it may not be so much that anyone is argued into it as much as it is absorbed unwittingly from the ambient culture. Even so, arguments do exist, and this one is squarely positioned on a scientific platform.

Morality too often gets in the way of freedom. It is becoming clearer that as societies evolve, certain moral restraints need to be relaxed or altogether stricken. No longer are they necessary for survival. In fact, they are frequently detrimental to personal fulfillment. In the earlier, more primitive stages of human evolution, social cohesiveness was critical to group survival. Small tribes in competition with other tribes for territory and scarce food resources, or striving to survive against nature itself, could not endure much diversity in behavior and lifestyle. Too much diversity might have caused the division of a tribe that might already have been challenged to maintain a critical mass of population. Social cohesion was critical for survival and necessarily depended on tight reigns over the behavior of individuals. A widespread practice of abortion, or a same-sex faction, might well have been catastrophic to a small primitive community—the continued existence of which depended on maximizing the number of offspring. Even a common practice of divorce might have seriously compromised a tribe's ability to cohere and to produce descendants fit for the challenges of survival in an uncivilized environment.

Restraints on behavior were found to be most effectively enforced by means of religious beliefs involving supernatural entities and associated notions of eternal punishment and reward systems. The study of primitive cultures of the past and those that exist today has shown that religious beliefs were and are central to their cohesiveness and thus to their survival. But today's advanced civilizations are not endangered by the same threats that imperiled early associations of Homo sapiens. If anything, overpopulation is now the looming threat, not extinction. Moral restraints necessary for survival in the evolutionary past are now merely extraneous and, to a great extent, even regressive. If the no longer purposeful appendix causes adverse symptoms threatening the well-being of the individual, it is surgically removed. Likewise, the evolutionary vestiges of social restrictions should be removed. If certain now-extraneous concepts of morality and their associated religious enforcement devices were removed from society, people would be freed up to choose among more diverse means of self-fulfillment. Who could deny that the more widespread the experience of self-fulfillment and well-being of individuals, the greater the collective well-being of society?

Religious beliefs upon which the past emphasis on morality depends have never been more than myths and stories; such belief systems cannot be proven by scientific methods. In fact, science has altogether disproven them, particularly the origin myths and legends that invariably accompany religious beliefs. Science has shown the origin myths and stories to be just that, myths and stories. Moreover, while the conformity to group thinking that religion produces was essential to survival in the past, it also blinds individuals to rationality and objectivity. Individuals caught up in or indoctrinated in patterns of groupthink and confirmation bias involving prospects of eternal rewards that so characterize religious beliefs are unable to think independently and critically. People lose the ability to think clearly about a subject once it is held as sacred.

It becomes necessary to ask, therefore, whether there is really any difference between morality and social convention. Is there any reason to think that there are right and wrong behaviors beyond localized cultural norms? The dizzying array of behavioral customs in the diverse cultures around the globe proves the point. So if nature has evolved to produce human beings as science has proven and there is no supernatural despot threatening eternal damnation, then moral rules are a matter of social consensus and convention, not something handed down from on high. This further means that religious people cannot be entrusted with moral determinations. Who are they to say what is right and wrong for everyone else? It remains for those unburdened by religious indoctrination to objectively point the way to changes in social conventions that would further the interest of modern advanced societies to fully realize human potential.

In the broadest terms, fairness and the prevention of harm to others are the highest standards of modern society. Thus, social and economic equality are the highest goals. But some social groups, whether they are distinguished by race, gender, nationality, ethnicity, or alternate orientations, do not always get a fair deal. They become victims of oppression by what has been the dominant group in a culture's history. The result has been religious arrogance, bigotry, intolerance, and stagnation of social reform, a hindrance to vibrant civilizations. Moral injunctions have been and often still are wielded as mechanisms of oppression. Wherever moral injunctions are imposed on behaviors that do not harm others, it is clear that one faction of society is applying them in order to maintain their position of superiority and dominance. Conventional religion tramples on the freedom of individuals and violates their rights. Thus, the path to real freedom is to diversify and dilute religion, subjugating its once-dominant strains, and where possible, to get rid of it.

Instead of being hinged to imagined deities, ethics must be thought of as bound to consensus. The process of settling upon ethical precepts and cultural norms is a collective project. It runs as a more or less semi-conscious enterprise operating within relationships and institutions. The myriad of focal points represented by each individual's perception of their own needs and the needs of society direct its progress. The only requirement for participation in the consensus building project is that no one insists on clinging to an authoritative ethical order from some mythical Mount Sinai beyond the reach of editing. Most importantly, the settlement is never static but constantly shifting, occasionally lurching, always being fashioned and conditioned according to the perceived needs of an evolving society. Ethical precepts and cultural norms are inventions, not discoveries; moral truth is not a standard against which such ideas are measured. Rather, moral truth emerges out of the consensus enterprise as ideas earn the right to be heard and to become positioned as common points of reference in a society's ethical landscape.

To summarize, religious myths and stories at one time lent justification to codes of behavior necessary for survival. Now it is clear from the findings of anthropology, psychology, and sociology that many of the moral restrictions these stories defend have outlived their utility and are merely oppressive. The suppression of natural tendencies and desires is harmful to individual self-expression and self-fulfillment and to the continued evolution of societies. Such taboos may now be safely removed from the present scientifically enlightened state of civilization.

The First to Present His Case Seems Right[1]

"Ah yes, the new morality. We adjust it according to the needs of an evolving society. It is a sin to call anything a sin. Sin is anything that hinders diversity and stagnates the flourishing of society," they say. Humanist philosopher Philip Kitcher's term *socially embedded normative guidance* aptly describes the ethical "project."[2] Accordingly, the sense of right and wrong is acquired through social interaction. Ethical precepts are imagined to find their form in the exchange of ethical opinions among our more socially engaged individuals, evolving over time as the flourishing of society requires.

A tidy picture, no doubt. But is it true? Resolution of the slavery-in-the-territories question by war would seem to have been at variance with socially embedded normative guidance. The ferocity of the sense of just and unjust exhibited in that and other such conflicts, in any case, might suggest something more about the origination of that sense than humanists would be pleased to acknowledge. Why do human beings not just operate on instinct as the animal kingdom seems to do? Would that not be much cleaner? Why is there this pesky knowledge of good and evil? What is the point of this knowledge being so dangerously accompanied by rationality and autonomy? Much of the time, this combination is managed poorly. Why do human beings plot and scheme when nothing else does? The purpose of these extra ingredients (knowledge of good and evil, rationality, and autonomy) is one of those questions that never seem to get very much attention, though the lack of attention may not be entirely disassociated from the poor management. We will venture into that territory before the end of the book. For now, it is necessary to take a look at what props up the new morality.

When one reasons on a false premise, it should be anticipated that whatever conclusions may be drawn are likely false. Scientific naturalism is a false premise. It is false because of the tacit admission that, along with everything else, the mind may be accounted for as an effect of natural causes. Herein lurks a contradiction: if scientific naturalism is a conclusion of rational inquiry, it is not an effect of natural causes. Yet, all the while scientific naturalism is true there is nothing that does not arise from natural causes.

We could suppose for a moment that a belief (such as scientific naturalism) *is* the effect of a cause originating in nature. But in registering it as an effect of a natural process, we are removing it as a conclusion of a rational process. A belief cannot originate as both an effect and a conclusion; as soon as it is attributable to events or conditions in the natural world, any rational grounds it might have enjoyed become irrelevant. The belief would have to exist whether there were rational grounds or not. The very fact that reasons are advanced in defense of a belief, whatever it may be, means that arguers implicitly acknowledge that it stands or falls upon reasons, not causes. It is reasons that are bantered about, not causes—reasons to accept or reasons to reject the belief. If beliefs were really matters of cause and effect, arguers would rather be applying "natural" selection processes on each other, that is, to forcibly expunge beliefs they deem unworthy of survival. That would be something more along the lines of what communist re-education camps do. But to their credit, promoters of scientific naturalism and evolutionism really do advance reasoned arguments. Scientific naturalism has, at least to this point, been defended and advanced by evidence and reasoning and not by silencing the holders of opposing views according to its own survival-of-the-fittest doctrine. I have not yet known an instance where an attempt has been made to eliminate disbelief in scientific naturalism by means of causes whose legality might be questioned—and hope I never do.

It is true that science is rational; it achieves its gains in part through rational inference, even if it should operate on a false premise. So how might nature have produced a creature capable of this mental activity of rationally drawing conclusions from consideration of evidence? Did this come about by chance? By the laws of nature? What kind of a process is rational inquiry anyway? Whatever it is, in view of the success of science overall, it does seem to be something that is able to put the ways of nature into its pocket, to leverage and control them to its own advantage, so it should not be out of place to call it *super*natural.

Many aspects of everyday experience are similar to rationality in their detachment from the cause-effect world. Such aspects of day-to-day living include truth, justice, meaning, purpose, goodness, freedom, love, hope, trust, and the fact that valuations are made. None of these life-worth-living attributes fall out of a scientific account of reality. Indeed, science bypasses them, not finding them productive fields of inquiry. They are natural only in the sense of being common; everyone lives in them, through them, and for them. To classify them as effects of biological causes nullifies their significance rather than explains it. In fact, their opposites—deceit, injustice, pointlessness, futility, evil, slavery, conceit, hopelessness, and suspicion—would have to be attributed to nature equally. If, then, the opposites are also biological effects, what more can be said about them? Plenty. But science is not equipped to make such judgments. It cannot even deal with the ethical implications of its own research, such as deciding whether to use or refrain from using atomic weaponry or genetic engineering. As with conflicting beliefs about reality, whenever one person's idea of good is found to be someone else's idea of evil, scientific naturalism can find in its domain only natural selection to mediate between them.

The word *norm* is a favorite of researchers undertaking to account for how the moral sense originated. It is a favorite term because of their presupposition that morality is a set of conformities adapted by social groups; it has nothing to do with objective values—values that they deem not to exist. Use of the word *taboo* to describe moral injunctions that researchers consider unenlightened, is another because it evokes images of primitive, superstitious cultures, thereby indicating that at least some aspects of morality have outlived their utility. Indeed, evolutionary utility would seem to be the only possible account for morality, which has surely, according to their presuppositions, evolved with the species.

Research into the supposed evolutionary origin and development of the moral sense thus regards the general mass of people as laboratory animals of sorts, as genetic survival modules. Any subject's actions are explainable, in total, as the result of gene selection and associated behavioral instincts that have proven to be evolutionarily advantageous. Yet the researchers themselves have somehow (they never think that they ought to explain it) risen above that to talk about real good and real evil. On what basis do they recommend generosity and kindness over selfishness and competition (and they do, same as anyone else) if the only possible cause for behavior is survival-based gene selection? They have to somehow equate morality with survival or else they are sunk.

Not to worry; they have that figured out. They can shift the focus to groups instead of individuals. In the midst of inter-group competition, groups gain survival advantages through internal cooperation. Morality, they speculate, was an evolutionary adaptation to enhance group cohesion, suppress self-interest, and maintain shared protocols, better enabling groups to cooperate and survive in competition with other groups.[3] In this, generosity, kindness, and reciprocity (the golden rule) suddenly become self-interested, group-based survival mechanisms. Nevertheless, instincts are instincts, so it is telling that these speculators yet still judge between individual-level, self-centered survival instincts and group-based, altruistic survival instincts.

Worse, reason is alleged to have evolved as a reputation-enhancing mechanism to further one's social standing and nothing more. This conclusion is drawn from scientific research that commonly finds intuition or passion ruling one's moral judgments, while reason attempts to justify, after the fact, what intuition or passion is already committed to.[4] The idea is that reasoning generates an enhanced reputation within the social group and an enhanced reputation leads to more offspring. And this all the while reason is applied to arrive at these disinterested scientific conclusions, that is, reasoning to the "truth" that reason is not "designed" to discover truth.

The language of evolutionary research may also include terms such as *groupthink* and *confirmation bias*. These terms can be useful in their descriptions of the origination of religion. Researchers ought to be more cautious though because someone might figure out that these terms can be sent back. Is it yet impossible for those caught up in the groupthink of scientific naturalism to have loosened their grasp on rationality and objectivity? Is scientific naturalism yet immune from being held sacred after the fashion of primitive idolatry? Is there not a confirmation bias with a view to freedom from moral accountability? If it is accountability they are attempting to dodge, the researchers quite obviously have good reason for trying to persuade themselves of a materialistic conception of the mind.

Playing Games with Values

Science delivers facts. Values are not facts. This is the so-called fact-value dichotomy, that great division of watersheds in Western civilization since the eighteenth century Enlightenment era. Values are not facts because value is not an inherent property of anything, either object or concept; rather, value is assigned. As individuals assign value differently, civilization is stuck with hashing out conflicts over the prioritization of values, over what should get more value and what should get less in public decision-making. A value-free society or a state of value neutrality is impossible; some values must prevail over others. Governments prioritize all the time, as do cultures and individuals. All governments aim to achieve societal effects that either they or their citizens collectively value. If nothing is valued, nothing is done.

Not everyone is always 100 percent satisfied with present states of society, and many look for progress toward greater freedom, equality, and justice. However, in order for some changes to occur, some reprioritizing of values needs to take place in people's minds, and there are sources of resistance. Because of the association that religion has to values and because religious beliefs tend to remain fixed, religion can often be a hindrance to achieving progress. The cultural authority of religion must be suppressed and, if possible, eliminated for some changes to move forward. That no one should have someone else's intolerant morality imposed on them, especially on their initiatives in diversification, is a chief reason for driving change. There is no need to directly confront entrenched religious resistance though; there are means to more subtly leverage reprioritizations of values below the level of general awareness.

A recent case in point involved a newfound right of universal free birth control assuming precedence over the longstanding right of free exercise of religion. Under the authority of the healthcare legislation of 2010, the executive branch directed that free contraceptives be made available to female participants in employer health benefit plans. By any reasonable measure, contraceptives are not a necessary provision for employee health, and thus, some employers took liberty to object to this regulation on religious grounds. Whether or not employees used contraceptives was of no concern to them. In fact, they did not wish to be forced to make that their concern by having to provide contraceptive services. Moreover, it was against their religious beliefs to supply certain forms of after-the-fact contraception called abortifacients. These are drugs that cause abortion in the earliest stage of pregnancy. There was a conflict, then, between the right of the free exercise of religion guaranteed by the First Amendment and the newly discovered right of universal birth control where it was suddenly felt that everyone is entitled to free contraceptives as much as they are entitled to breathe air. It is unfortunate, but free contraceptives need to be paid for by someone, and some of those targeted as suppliers were those whose observance of their religion would forbid them. But surely so trivial a matter as outdated religious scruples cannot stand in the way of progress. Here was an instance of the value of the centuries-long campaign for the free exercise of religion being set aside so that a previously unrecognized value could rule. The change was justified on the grounds that what was formerly an optional activity with certain risks was now one in which risk-free indulgence (i.e., with birth control) was to be regarded as a right. The subtlety was in how the new right was staged as if its superiority was already plainly obvious to any casual bystander.[5]

The strategy to achieve cultural change is to first elevate public awareness of a new value or right, marginalize moral objections as against progress, freedom, and rights, then continue to press the newly valued behavior into the culture through entertainment and news media and public education as something normal. By so doing, one value is elevated or amplified in order to overshadow or subordinate another. In this fashion, divorce was normalized and made to be seen as a legitimate and socially accepted practice. It once was not. The values of individual autonomy and prerogative were elevated and amplified. It is not that the values being elevated were unimportant or unworthy; they are worthy values. But here, the value of marriage and family to the building of integrity and loyalty was denied a voice so that these other values could occupy the stage. Relaxing of the burden of proof for establishing grounds for divorce in state laws by no-fault divorce was the result—a presumed triumph of progress, freedom, and rights.

The practice of abortion was likewise normalized. Normalization was achieved similarly in this instance by stressing the right of privacy, and later the right of liberty as any individual might wish to define it (see chapter 2, the debate over judicial review). Relief from the unequal reproductive burden was also involved. The value of life of the unborn was subordinated. Thus, as a private matter of individual liberty, certain people now have the legal right to decide, within certain boundaries, who lives and who dies. Here, newly devised rights having dubious constitutional backing have effectively nullified the God-given right of life upheld in the Declaration of Independence. (It hardly needs to be mentioned what further appalling consequences would follow if the rights of privacy and liberty, as personally defined, were to prevail over that of life in other domains.) Similar to divorce, abortion was once understood to be morally suspect enough to have either restrictions or prohibitions encoded in state laws. Reasons as to why that might no longer be the case were thought unnecessary; there was to be acknowledged only the "higher" values of privacy and liberty as personally defined in the public resolution. State laws were thereby unconstitutionalized in the name of progress, freedom, and rights.

Similarly, in regard to same-sex relationships, the values of equality and non-discrimination were elevated. Though in contrast to abortion, which is itself actively concealed from public view, this alternative arrangement was set on stage by entertainment media and public education propaganda campaigns as something natural and normal.[6] A specific goal was to force awareness on those who rather would have preferred to remain excused from such awareness. Through the portrayal of the practice as natural and normal, whatever reservations there might have been as to its propriety were dismissed. Any disfavor was declared to be discriminatory—end of discussion. The values of equality and non-discrimination were amplified over the value and sanctity of marriage so that associations more properly characterized as disoriented than alternately oriented—that is, if nature would have been consulted—are worthy of the same honor. Equality and non-discrimination are legitimate values in themselves, but they are misapplied in this instance. They are misapplied because there are justifiable reservations against recognition of same-sex associations. It is not a phobia that those who object on religious grounds are afflicted with. It is revulsion that a practice that defies and heaps contempt on the Creator's design and intention should be made public as if somehow respectable.

The subtlety of the value manipulation game is in how a given conflict is staged or framed for resolution in the court of public opinion. How a value conflict is framed determines what is relevant to it and very often how it is going to be resolved. Framing narrows a conflict to a question involving one specific value or right—equality, privacy, or individual autonomy in the cases already mentioned. Narrowing is easy to accomplish through entertainment and news media and public education. All they need to do is present the narrow view consistently. All other considerations, especially moral objections and sensibilities, are either not permitted a public voice or else dismissed in fits of indignation and labeling, including charges of bigotry, narrow-mindedness, phobia, ignorance, and anti-science. Whoever can cause their particular staging of the conflict to prevail in public opinion is whose view rules. By so doing, the change agents' preferred resolution may be pretty well assured by the time the matter is heard in court.

The above cultural changes do not by themselves appear to have caused extensive damage to individual rights, except whatever right might have been retained by the unborn. Rights of conscience and speech are still pretty much intact, for now. Though there are some exceptions and disconcerting trends, people are not generally being compelled by threats and penalties to comply, against conscience, with some practice or to assent to some belief. Though the wielders of the concepts of hate crimes and hate speech are ever more anxious to apply this their condemnatory instrument and though managers of public forums are ever more intent on using the same as a basis for exclusion, there are not yet widespread threats and penalties against political and religious speech opposing the imposition of power gamer morality. Government is still a spectator generally. Moreover, there is never a time when cultural changes are not going on, so why the fuss? If many want to be freed up to do their thing, then so what? Where are the adverse consequences?

It may be that adverse consequences are nonexistent. But maybe they are just not immediately apparent. Suppose adverse consequences do not become evident until later. Suppose they appear in subsequent generations and are not easy to foresee. What is required to raise a child up into adulthood, instilling meaning and purpose, senses of goodness and justice, self-reliance and self-control, integrity and trustworthiness? Are these necessities served by abandoned commitment, convenient disposal, and shameless display? Who will turn the hearts of the fathers to the children?[7] Granted, neither arguments from consequences nor those in defense of the reality of the Creator and the reverence due advanced against self-interested cultural changes are likely to reverse their course. The power gamers are unaware of their self-degradation.[8] Surely not the least objectionable turn of events, though, is how the courts, in their justifications, have disgraced the Constitution, an honorable document, and wise. They have read into the Constitution the basest of liberties.

The value manipulation game can be worked on both sides of any conflict. But it is clear that those who object to standards of morality really just want to impose their own version of morality. The hypocrisy of forcing reprioritizations is in the fact that the argument used against the values being replaced or subordinated is that no one should be imposing their values on someone else. Universal tolerance is demanded. Then, in the name of equality, freedom, and rights, a new version of morality, a revised set of do's and don'ts, is imposed on everyone else. The real question is never whether morality will be imposed but what morality will be imposed.

Erosion of Liberty: Whose Values Shall Apply?

Disassociating the administration of justice from transcendence does not leave secular society scrambling for principles on which to form a just society. But it does leave the administration somewhat diminished. Gone as irrelevant are honesty, integrity, loyalty, and deference to authority. Honesty and integrity tend to yield too greatly to the possibility that moral truth exists independent of what anyone may happen to believe about it. Loyalty and deference to authority are too suggestive of hierarchy and thus inequality. These are virtues that have little use in a world that stresses moral self-determination, that is, where everyone gets to make up their own rules. The external appearance of a just society, fairness and absence of harm, remain;

and equality and toleration tend to float to the top of the list of virtues because these are... well... what remain on the list.

It is easy to define the ideal condition of society in terms of equality; equalization makes as much or more pretense to producing overall harmony and happiness as anything else. The meaning of equality here does not stop at equal protection of the laws; to the degree that it is an ideal, equality is not truly satisfied until it moves on to uniformity of economic status and social standing. Economic and social equality leave nothing to covet or envy. Differing beliefs must be of equal value because for some beliefs to be regarded as inferior might suggest the same about those who hold them. The secularization, pluralization, and privatization described in chapter 3 and the postmodernism described in chapter 4 wherein all assessments of belief as true or false are inadmissible, gain traction on this point. Levelization opens the door to diversity because nothing is to be rejected; and lots of diversity requires lots of tolerance. It is all very democratic.

Justice in the form of equality, diversity, and toleration does have much to commend itself, and there is much good to be found. Past agents of equality, diversity, and toleration include Roger Williams and William Penn in the toleration of religious differences, the English barons of 1215 and John Locke in equalization under the rule of law and natural rights, Thomas Jefferson and the Continental Congress in the separate and equal station of a people among the powers of the earth, James Madison and the first congress under the Constitution in equality of conscience through the disestablishment and free exercise of religion, Abraham Lincoln and the Republicans in the Emancipation Proclamation and the repudiation of slavery, and chief justice Earl Warren and the 1954 *Brown v. Board of Education* Supreme Court in removal of the inequalities of segregation.[9] These advances of civilization arising from belief in the equal station of persons have had few equals.

But equality of persons is not the only achievement brought about by the elevation of equality, diversity, and toleration. If secular society has sought to gain something over religion, it has found it here. Equality, diversity, and toleration are enlightened, egalitarian, and magnanimous. The superiority of secular culture is in how much more tolerant, accepting, and equality-minded it is. Without actually saying so, what equality, diversity, and toleration presume to gain for secularism is the moral high ground over traditional religious virtues. It is because traditional morality is not terribly diverse, not open to revision, and not given to an abundance of toleration. But in striving after universal acceptance, what the equality-diversity-toleration community becomes is the very thing it deplores. As much as moral objectivity and discernment is detested and disowned, moral fixation returns with a vengeance—bigotry, narrow-mindedness, and intolerance overtake the very champions of equality, diversity, and toleration. The return is manifested against anyone who thinks that not everything is equal and tolerable. It is seen in obsession with and exclusion against "unenlightened" speech—speech not entirely in harmony with the tune of equality, diversity, and toleration. Daring to uphold traditional values such as the superiority of the traditional family over various lifestyle alternatives, or the priority of natural rights such as the right of conscience over government-invented rights such as free birth control, are examples. In this, the intolerance of universal tolerance becomes evident: non-tolerance is intolerable to those who like to think of themselves as the most tolerant.

No religion is so petty and doctrinaire as political correctness. It makes a pretense to enjoining acceptance and opposing discrimination, but as the exercise of power is its means of commending itself, discrimination and intimidation are what it does. Who does not resent having religion imposed on them? That, however, is what happens. More naive secularists think they are doing away with religion. They do not get rid of it. Religion is not done away, only replaced. Secularization allows the religion of political correctness—the pursuit of freedom from exposure to contrary views by the "most tolerant"—to gain control over the public space. Consent is more closely prescribed and natural rights of conscience and speech are more closely regulated. Equality, diversity, and toleration supply a sure base for leveraging the power of condemnation against traditional forms of religion. But political correctness is a religion so paltry that it has no basis to condemn even the gunman mayhem that has recently become all too common in public schools and public gathering places. Because even gunman values and concepts of existence have to be tolerated, it has to borrow (selectively, of course) from traditional morality (Do not murder) to issue condemnations in such instances.

The impossibility of achieving a universally tolerant society means that tolerance is applied selectively. Be forewarned, then, should loud-speaking proponents of specialized versions of equality and diversity, in their insecurity and anxiety over possible deviations of opinion, begin to petition government to enforce them. No secularized society has access to the domain that answers why there is knowledge of good and evil in the first place. And no more favorable invitation for the reformulation of justice exists than when it appears that conscience has no transcendent roots, cannot be rationally appraised, and moral judgments have no objective content. Thus, the sense of right and wrong (acute though it may be) is at best a cultural phenomenon. Having thrown out the only rational basis for value priorities, the laws of nature and nature's God, the remaining bases of ordering them are limited to cultures and persons. An unwary populace is then vulnerable to the subtle and deceitful elevating of one value to suppress another and the denial of opportunity for conscience to weigh in. After obliterating their own consciences, it seems that the proponents of political religion must have everyone else's obliterated too.

When truth is not sought-after and honored, justice is turned back from the face of power, and power makes conscience its prey. It is the sort of "freedom" you get in a godless world.

CHAPTER 6

LIBERTY REVISITED

But I preferred to do nothing without your consent in order that your goodness might not be by compulsion but of your own free will.

—Philemon 14, RSV

Dismissing Incompatible Ideologies

Before further progress can be made toward an appreciation of liberty, two incompatible ideologies need to be confronted. Both viewpoints amount to a denial of free will. Liberty, though, must begin with free will—will that is self-determined and not ruled by outside causal factors. Any talk of liberty is pointless if there is no autonomy from natural or supernatural causes. One incompatible viewpoint is the philosophy of naturalism, which, to this point, has been called scientific naturalism and which may alternately be called scientific determinism. This viewpoint is the dependence of all things on natural causes. The other is a misrepresentation of divinity, the theology of Calvinism, the subjection of all things to supernatural will.

Naturalism is the denial of the existence of the supernatural. It leaves the natural world intact but with nothing outside of it. While science itself neither affirms nor denies the existence of a supernatural realm, the assumption of naturalism is a central working principle of scientific methods and a philosophical position promoted by many scientists. The scientist's cause-effect accounts are quite at home within this philosophy. Indeed, they are the only type of accounts that are. That is the difficulty with naturalism. If a scientific account of behavior is desired, a cause-effect account is the only type of account that can be advanced. Yet cause-effect explanations are incompatible with the autonomy from cause and effect that individuals must claim for themselves if the terms *liberty* or *freedom* are to have any meaning. Cause-effect processes are deterministic in that given the presence of causes, the associated effects are inevitable. Whatever the effects may be, they are explainable, in total, from the relevant causes. So, in a world ruled by cause and effect, there is no room for independence or autonomy from whatever might be the relevant causes. The scientific world of cause and effect defies the very essence of freedom. Scientists and philosophers who subscribe to the philosophy of naturalism rigorously either deny free will or else are baffled by it.

In philosophy, the question of whether or not human beings have free will is a problem posed for philosophical study. The existence of free will has been a major philosophical problem for much of Western civilization. It became acute during the seventeenth and eighteenth centuries with the triumph of the scientific revolution, and even more so as the philosophy of naturalism became intellectually viable with the subsequent success of evolutionary science in the nineteenth century. Yet, after all this time of being on the docket, the problem of free will remains a major philosophical conundrum. If there was an answer that would put the matter to rest, one would think it would have been found already.

As an abstract question posed about human beings in general, the question of free will is indeed unanswerable. It is impossible to draw from observation whether human beings have free will or not. The surface facts of behavior do not reveal whether natural causes may be acting internally or not. But it is possible to know whether persons have free will from the inside. And the answer arrives perhaps most clearly from what is demanded as an explanation of someone else's behavior. When any of us are offended by the behavior of another— and everyone has limits to what they will put up with—we do not demand a scientific explanation but a personal one. We take issue not with biochemistry, genetics, or society but with the person. And the reason that we reject a scientific account and require a personal acknowledgment and responsibility is that we know implicitly that we ourselves have autonomy. If we have autonomy, we expect that other human beings have it as well. Scientific determinism is not a viable philosophical position for this reason. The subject of human behavior is inaccessible to scientific methods, which is why it still resides in the domains of philosophy, even while psychology and sociology attempt to find statistical patterns in expectation that it is somehow predictable.

The other extreme philosophical position is the theology of Calvinism named after the sixteenth century Protestant reformer and theologian John Calvin (1509–64). Invariably, the question of free will arises in connection with Calvinist teachings. God is said to have predetermined, at the level of each individual, who will be saved and who will be condemned. Everyone is predestined either to salvation or damnation beforehand, and nothing that anyone does or can do is relevant to their status in that regard. Predestination is deduced from the central Calvinist premise of the absolute sovereignty of God. In this, divine will preempts individual will. In placing divine will as sovereign over that of the individual, one's eternal "election" becomes a divine determination and is granted unconditionally. With all the stress placed on personal freedom in the New Testament,[1] it is a wonder how theology can become so overcooked. All New Testament teaching bears on salvation and is an appeal to do one thing and not another, teaching that is meaningless outside of individual privilege.

As if absolute sovereignty were not enough, to further cement one's eternal destiny, the sovereignty of God premise is joined to an associated principle of Calvinist theology: Human beings are totally depraved and cannot do anything to commend themselves to the divine being apart from intercession of the divine being. Here, then, is removed perhaps the most important degree of freedom from persons— the ability to decide between doing good or doing evil. Only divine intercession, says the Calvinist, can elevate someone from their state of depravity. Only then can they do good. And once being interceded upon, they would be unable to do evil. Any account of behavior would seem necessarily to become a theological matter, whether or not divine intervention has been performed in someone's case. How one's election status is evident or relevant in day-to-day affairs is a question that invariably follows and Calvinist theology has much to say on this. Yet, be that as it may, sovereignty, predestination, and depravity still appear to leave free will standing outside the door. Therefore, even with all the original Protestant stress on vernacular translations and every person's need to follow the Bible, the whole Bible, and nothing but the Bible, the exalted book would seem altogether extraneous if God has predetermined who is in and who is out. All that remains is to try to figure out who is on which roster.

Calvinist apologists can be slippery, straddling a contradiction without appearing to do so. What is desired is certainty about one's eternal destiny. There is an exchange of freedom for an imagined security similar perhaps to that which drives socialism. But they do not want to appear to subscribe to the sort of fatalism that turns persons into automatons under the control of a master puppeteer. It is possible, then, to stipulate that some limited free will exists within the confines of divine will. And so yes, there might well be personal liberty within certain boundaries. The boundaries would be those that exclude affecting an individual's salvation status or commending one's self to the divine being. But what sort of boundaries would these be? Without means to commend one's self to the divine being or otherwise get out of their total depravity, how should anyone be able to commend one's self to anyone? Whatever degrees of liberty remain, then, after divine will has supposedly reserved its domain cannot involve choosing between good and evil and are likely to be of little consequence. If they should say you cannot have an incursion of free will into territory set aside for divine will, why did the Lord instruct His followers to pray "Thy will be done on earth as it is in heaven"[2]? It should be clear that not everything that happens on earth is according to His will. Given that it is not, the Lord's exhortation was to "strive to enter by the narrow door."[3] Whatever answers could and would be given to abstract questions such as the one immediately preceding ("Will those who are saved be few?") could never satisfy curiosity about one's own status. The abstract concept of predestination is no help at all.

In granting free will, the Almighty has chosen to limit the exercise of His sovereignty. In addition to abundant appeals of the scriptures themselves as to the exercise of free will, the downfall of Calvinism is the same as that of scientific determinism: the demand for personal responsibility indicates that responsibility rests within the person. A supernatural agent is not responsible. "The devil made me do it" or some more elaborate story involving supernatural manipulation is never accepted as an account of behavior. It is unnecessary and unwise to get further mired in the subtleties of Protestant theology. The takeaway is that a cloud of suspicion hangs over the Calvinist project by the mere fact that the question of free will even arises at all.

Scientific determinists and Calvinists attempt to persuade you to *voluntarily* drop your ideas about free will! Trying to salvage a scientific or Calvinist view of reality by denying free will is like throwing the baby out and keeping the bath water. It is the unpredictability of free will that makes the wonderful world of people so lively. However, it is not realistically probable that either scientific determinism or Calvinism will someday phase out. Those not identifying themselves as deterministic or Calvinistic or in agreement with any of the world's other fatalistic religions implicitly acknowledge free will and personal responsibility for words and actions. As much as responsibility may be ditched, it sooner or later arrives back at the doorstep of the person. Neither biochemistry, nor God, nor the devil is accepted as a responsible agent, say, in a court of law. Free will is understood to be one of the ground rules governing the conduct of the human being. There are no explanations for how it exists. The Bible does not explain how free will exists either; it only displays its existence. The third chapter of Genesis displays free will in straightforward fashion. In the remainder of the scriptures, free will is a given, and persuading mankind to turn to Him is the enterprise of God.

The Reality of Liberty

Though it is not an account of human behavior, the principle of cause and effect is a necessary precondition for free will to gain traction. Philosopher David Hume's (1711–76) skepticism about cause and effect being anything more than a habit of mind may be justifiable in the abstract. How could anyone decisively prove cause and effect to be a principle ruling the natural world—that occurrences in the world are always caused by preceding conditions and events? Why should one event necessarily *cause* another event? Perhaps events only exhibit temporal contiguity, where *B* consistently follows *A,* though *A* is never the cause of *B*. But that skepticism was sent fleeing by a common sense observation that professor Daniel N. Robinson attributes to philosopher Thomas Reid (1710–96).[4] Certainty about cause and effect is due to our being able to routinely insert extra-natural causes into the cause-effect world to produce effects that the natural world could never produce on its own. Any man-made object or natural object disturbed from its natural state is evidence of such cause insertion. In light of this observation, the inference to occurrences out in the world, that they also are caused, is straightforward. At the same time, while the principle of cause and effect is common sense, extra-natural insertions hint that there is more to existence than just that.

In a cause-effect ruled world open to insertions from the outside, means-ends thinking—that is, inferring the effects or ends from outside cause insertions or means—becomes possible. The ends anticipated to result from associated means are the purposes, intents, and designs of autonomous agents. The serpent's subtlety in such means-ends thinking is on display in Genesis chapter 3. The serpent approached Eve and said, "Did God really say, 'You must not eat from any tree in the garden?'"[5] The purpose of that insertion, of course, was to direct attention toward the prohibited tree knowing what would almost certainly follow. Modern advertising follows the same stratagem for good or for ill. All advertisers need to do is to redirect the prospect's attention, and their affection should not be far behind.

It is necessary, though, to consider what was really going on in the garden and just what was at risk. By testing the newly formed creature (mankind) over the matter of the tree of the knowledge of good and evil, the serpent (the devil) could determine whether it (the creature) had similar autonomy from the will of its creator as his own. The end in view for enticing the creature to turn against its creator was the possibility that the creature really would turn away. Prior rebellion of the devil is presupposed in the attempt. The test produced, from the devil's point of view, a positive result: the creature disregarded the warning and acquired the knowledge of good and evil. At that instant, participants in the rebellion were expanded to include the creature. Autonomy of the creature's will from that of its creator is unequivocally demonstrated in Genesis 3. For God to have played the creature into the serpent's scheme or to have directed the serpent's subsequent deceptive leading ("You will not surely die"), would have been self-contradictory. Now the contention between God and the devil would continue. It would continue to see which way the creature would finally turn.

Had Adam and Eve maintained their innocence, the entire creative enterprise might, for all appearances, have been merely a scripted stage play, no more than a diversion from the heavenly standoff resulting from the devil's rebellion. The creature's autonomy and free will would not have been apparent to an observer such as the devil. But now it was apparent. The point of the sequence of events just described may well have been to show it. Free will is at least the ground rule and necessary prerequisite for the introduction of something called love. Love can exist only if it is freely given.[6] No scripted or externally compelled response can attain to this quality. The range of possibilities must be meaningful as well; there is little significance in limiting the possibilities to goodness *A* or goodness *B*. In order for the possibility of love to continue, the door is open to evil. But it is love that raises the creature above the role of hostage in a deadly game. In this, the point of the creation hinges on the creature's free will. Without it, the creation is a pointless exhibition. Love really is *the* pivotal force and would later become the answer to the devil's rebellion.

The Creator's name was besmirched. It was besmirched not only by the offense of the serpent's rebellion but also by the fall of the creature and its subsequent descent into corruption. What was originally created good was now open to evil intent. This was not so much a consequence of the knowledge of good and evil itself. Rather, it was by the corruption of splendor and the desire to be like God. In enticing the creature to rebel, the devil had added, "Your eyes will be opened, and you will be like God, knowing good and evil."[7] Becoming like God was not the creature's privilege; it was the same mistake as the devil's.[8] The creature, in turning away from its Creator, was locked into a hopeless condition of being unable to maintain its original goodness. The package of acquired knowledge did not have in it the sort of power necessary to always decide for good. What power the creature did possess began to be applied for self-glorification, like the devil. Even when there was a choosing of the right and good, it was, being without faith, self-serving. Because of the evil that results from self-centeredness, there was just condemnation.[9] Such a creature could not be permitted to exist forever, and it would, as a consequence, be bound even more by its fear of death.[10] But the Creator did not begin an enterprise merely to hand it over to the enemy; a rescue operation had been planned also. That rescue operation—behind enemy lines—would procure not only the creature's freedom from its powerless condition but also the Creator's vindication. Now the tables would be turned; instead of free will being demonstrated by disobedience in a world under the power of God, it would be demonstrated by its opposite in a world ruled by the devil.[11]

The rescue operation is the topic of another book whose first scene has just been described in summary; there is no need to continue that here. The point is to lead to this question: Should the foregoing be linked up with what is known to be real—the knowledge of good and evil and the liberty or free will or autonomy to choose between them? No knowledge is as innate as the knowledge of good and evil. No instruction, indoctrination, justification, persuasion, or recommendation is necessary to establish the existence of good and evil as if a knowledge vacuum existed. The universal tendency is for persons to apply that knowledge against others, even while they themselves covertly do what they deem not acceptable when done by someone else.[12] The knowledge of good and evil is even applied as a ruse as if to disprove the existence of God. That is, the persuasiveness of arguments denying the existence of God is presumed to be proportional to the length and horror of the catalog of the world's evils. Unfortunately, a catalog of evils does not work to the benefit of the argument unless it is advanced as objective, as something that all parties are obliged to agree with. The catalog cannot be solely a complaint of the God disprover. The inference to transcendence from the reality of good and evil is not altogether inconceivable. In fact, it is inescapable.

The knowledge of good and evil and the liberty to choose between them must find a root in reality because the conflict between good and evil is real. Where shall one go to find that root? The possible locations are very few indeed. One thing is certain: the reality of personal liberty, and good and evil, is distinctly beyond the explanatory power of scientific naturalism.

Liberty and Means of Persuasion

The connection between truth and liberty may be illustrated in certain instances involving confrontation. John chapter 9 describes just such a confrontation involving a man who was blind from birth and whose sight the Lord Jesus had just restored. Here are the actors: God; those who play God; those for whom a relevant fact or a conclusion drawn from evidence rules; and those who float along with the currents, having absorbed their beliefs and convictions from the ambient culture. That Jesus restored the man's sight demonstrated that He was from God. The Pharisees, having assumed the role of God, questioned the miracle. Refusing to accept the testimony of others that a miracle had been performed, they made known that if anyone ventured to acknowledge Jesus instead of themselves as the agents of God, they would be put to public disrepute and exclusion by being cast out of the synagogue. The formerly blind man recognized the power of Jesus over sight, concluded that he was from God, and stood on that conclusion against the Pharisees' less-than-honest questioning. "If this man were not from God, he could do nothing" he said.[13] The formerly blind received for his trouble the pre-specified compensation; he was cast out. In contrast, the parents and neighbors of the man who had been blind were sensitive to pressure to conform and dared not resist the currents of correctness.

There is no argument needed that God is at liberty: "He does whatever He pleases."[14] Nor is it necessary to argue for the liberty of the Pharisees; it appeared that they could do whatever they pleased. The formerly blind was under penalty and restriction, the price of spiritual sight. The parents and neighbors remained unconstrained, or so they thought. The question is who was at liberty, the parents and neighbors or the man formerly blind?

A subsequent confrontation in John chapter 18 varies slightly from chapter 9, though significantly. Here, it was Jesus, the Son of God, who assumed the role of one who stands on truth and pays for the privilege. Again, it became necessary for the religious leaders as "agents of God" to apply coercive measures to make sure that the correct outcome was obtained: no man shall claim to be God. Though they could not take direct action in this instance, they stirred up a boisterous crowd to pressure the governor to comply with their demand regarding the defendant Jesus, whom they had thrust at to dispose of. The chief priests knew that as guardian of civil order, for a disturbance to arise under a governor's watch would be a check against his professional record. The overseers of the empire were very sensitive to public disturbances. A conversation between the governor and Jesus about Jesus's identity is reported at the end of which the governor asks, "What is truth?"[15] He did not stand by for an answer. Circumstances being what they were, what truth was, was not nearly so relevant to the governor as his being able to dodge the inconvenience and personal cost of defending it. Again, who was at liberty, the governor or Jesus? Tilting of the motivational landscape in such fashion as to direct the course of responses might begin merely as a bribe. But the slope of injustice has often been increased by including inconvenience, slander, ridicule, imprisonment, violent harm, and death. In this instance, the Son of God, in calm resolution befitting divinity, would not deny His identity.

The ground rules are that physical laws of nature are inviolable. But laws governing spirits are not; they may be transgressed or left unfulfilled. Truth and liberty stand or fall in confrontations between spirits. To be buyable, or for one's allegiance to the true and right to be up for sale or subject to pressure to conform, is to give way and lose both truth and liberty. Does virtue not resist such pressure? Does real liberty, despite what some may say, not require virtue?

There is conventional freedom in God's world; the commandments are few. After recounting the utterance of the Ten Commandments by Almighty God from Mount Sinai, Moses reassured the Israelites, saying, "And He added no more."[16] Not only did He add no more, the Almighty allows individuals and nations to drift or rebel even from these few commandments rather than constrain their will. He could terrify everyone into compliance by His presence, or intervene against free will to prevent violations of laws governing spirits, but does not. The prophets pleaded with Israel for hundreds of years to turn back from their waywardness. These pleadings were not threats; they were warnings. In this, the I AM is seen to be on the side of liberty and reasoned persuasion, not coercion. In the finality of His judgment and terrifying majesty, as once experienced at Mt. Sinai and as declared by the unfathomable universe, the I AM removes Himself from view to allow space for reasoned appeal, for liberty, to allow inquiry into truth, if anyone might want it.

Reason is more than a tool of self-justification; it is the path to truth, even if rarely applied for that purpose. Its use for truth is also the certificate of a nation's liberty. Yes, the readiest indicator of the presence of truth and liberty may not be as much truth and liberty themselves as the means of persuasion in common use. The distinction between reasoned and coercive means of persuasion is pivotal. It is the difference between those who have a case and those who do not. To say that the pinnacle of Western civilization has been the elevation of reasoned persuasion over coercion may not be an overstatement. The measure of a civilization may well be found in its means of persuasion and the right to remain unconvinced by someone else's great ideas (including ideas in this book).

Though the I AM allows space for reasoned inquiry, others too often rush in to fill it with something else. The reason-requires-liberty corner of the square of liberty is easily interrupted. The interruption is felt in the suppression of whatever reasoned appeal is out of fashion and the casting of that appeal into disrepute. In his first inaugural address, Thomas Jefferson said, "Error of opinion may be tolerated where reason is left free to combat it." But even if reason is not left free to combat it, there is still liberty. There is still the liberty that springs from virtue that springs from the fact that God is and has spoken. The real question may not be so much whether God exists. He may well exist all the while it is easy to disregard that existence. The real question is whether He has spoken. The sort of liberty that defies coercion needs backing; backing requires truth. Truth will finally require the words of God because only they are incorruptible and immovable.

Is the United States a Christian Nation?

It would be a mistake to think that any nation could exist officially as a Christian nation. After the fashion of its founder, Christianity is flatly not interested in political rule.[17] Though there is no prohibition in the Bible against individual Christians participating in government—they are free to aspire to and to fill public offices—for what might nominally be regarded as a church of Christianity to assume some role in political governance or in government regulation of belief disqualifies it as having anything to do with Christianity.[18] In answer, then, as to whether the United States is a Christian nation, it can, at most, be said in certain of its principles indirectly. The United States was founded on natural law principles, specifically making natural right central. Natural right was a focal point of Enlightenment era thought. But it also happens to be consistent with the second table of the Ten Commandments. The consistency is seen in how the commandments, in addition to establishing the sacredness of a person's trust and reputation, uphold individual rights of life and property. The Declaration of Independence almost connected the dots.

As much as this point about natural right and commandments six through ten is obscured, a second point may be even more critical to liberty and is even more obscured: the first table of the Ten Commandments separates God and government. The fact of an authority that is not government, and for which government is prohibited from being a substitute, is reflected in "Thou shall have no other gods before me." Government cannot take the place of

God. If, however, the general opinion is that God does not exist, then government might well aspire to become, in effect, God. Pursuit of an ideal or utopian state assures that it will even more.

Therefore, the wall separating church and state must exist. But it cannot be total. A total wall is the complete secularization of the public space where anything that resembles a conventional religious belief is banished. This is where government can eye the opportunity to act as God and seize it, or else if a majority or loud minority wants the government to act as God to align everyone else with its views, the government can oblige. There are examples of this now and in the past. On the opposite end, no wall is unification of religion and state, when religion owns government or government owns religion, which is the same as government becoming God. There are examples of that as well. There is no real difference between total wall and no wall. If free citizens are unable to traverse and maintain the reasoned pathways necessary to identify the Creator, if they continue to be unmotivated or unable to work through the metaphysics, they may fall into a state of confusion and accept misrepresentations about the Creator or deny the Creator altogether. They will certainly lose the benefit of absolute claims against others and against governments for their rights, and possibly also the equal applicability and protection of law.

Voluntary consent to a higher authority that is not government is the essence of self-government and liberty. Without voluntary consent, it is coercion. Without a higher authority, there is only the conflict of opinions, which begets coercion. Citizens need to figure out that they are under the authority of God. If they are able to figure that out, they will require public officials to govern in a manner consistent with divine rightness, goodness, and justice. They will also resist subtle influences that weaken a people's resolve against totalitarian advances. In this they will ignore the entertainment industry's attempts to saturate the culture with materialism, degeneracy, and trivialities. They will discern the major news media's inordinate control over the public agenda and discount its filtering of content according to its preconceived standards of correctness. And they will abandon public education with its disregard of American constitutional principles and legacy and its selective prohibitions against distinctions between good and evil. Further, they will reassert their responsibility for educating their offspring, personally exemplifying for them the character and excellence of their Creator. In this, they will stand against attempts by the cultural gatekeepers to falsify or degrade what is true, right, and just. This is the hard idea of liberty. Who shall finally set the rules? *God, self-existent, exalted, incorruptible, though just out of range of perception and easily ignored or forgotten, when revered by the people, puts the weightiest of all checks and balances on overbearing authority, including government.*

CHAPTER 7

WRITING ON THE WALL

But the God in whose hand is your breath, and whose are all your ways, you have not honored
　　　　　　　　　　　　　　　　　　—Daniel 5:23, RSV

The wall of separation between church and state, alleged to be justified by fact-value, reason-faith, and public-private divides, may not be so "high and impregnable"1 as those who enforce it like to imagine. The more such separations are enforced, the more an assortment of hypocrisies emerges, even if largely unrecognized. It is because those who think of themselves as planted on the fact/reason/ public side of the wall quite expect their supposed facts and reasoning to be valued and believed and not just in private.

What should be said about the professors who believe in the value of their own lives and are in a fuss when some gunman shoots up a school, but in their classrooms insinuate that there is no objective reference for value and belief?

What should be said about the secularists who think that liberty is gained by clearing the public space of transcendent moral coordinates all the while scheming to establish their own substitute coordinates?

What should be said about the academics who, with a pretense of good intention in thinking to protect everyone from the error of religious beliefs, belittle the supernatural all the while failing to recognize that neither goodness nor intention can exist without it?

What should be said about the moralists who denounce anyone who would impose their values on someone else yet who, in their very denunciation, impose the value of withholding judgment on everyone else? Seldom even are they content to stop at that but go on to impose values of the political religion and its dogma of equality of beliefs at the expense of truth on everyone else.

What should be said about judges, especially Supreme Court justices who believe that for public educational institutions to uphold Creator-endowed rights encoded in the First Amendment means wielding the First Amendment to strike out acknowledgment of the Creator?

What should be said about journalists who suppose themselves to be champions of objectivity and truth all the while positioned as gate-keepers of public discourse by what they subjectively and often dishonestly allow to filter through their media outlets? In setting the parameters of culture and the dictates of correctness, they become imprisoned in their own biases, hostile to larger realities.

Maybe values and beliefs are not so private after all. In fact, there are so many tacit exceptions to privatization that it is a wonder that the secular duplicity goes so unnoticed. Religion, remember, is not done away within the public space, only replaced. Like the Pharisees of old, these religious leaders of today similarly radiate their values and beliefs into it. Their values and beliefs flood through the channels of education, news, and entertainment; they are "in the air." In their acquisition of knowledge (epistemology) and discernment of good and evil (ethics), these religious leaders glory in the power of their own minds. But all the while acquiring and discerning, they suppress the honest conclusions of epistemology and ethics that they cannot be the authors of their own minds.

Can the intellectual and moral capacities be anything other than loaned capacities? No one invents them or owns them such as to pronounce their obligations and constraints. Though the religious leaders strive to gain a measure of control because of the immense power that knowledge and a basis of condemnation give them, they learned the obligations and constraints of logos and ethos like everyone else, often through mistakes. Alas, for the religious leaders of today. As their days count down, the horizon within which they can fulfill their secularizing stratagems and enjoy the fruits is ever diminishing. They should rather "seek the Lord, if haply they might feel after him, and find him, though he be not far from every one of us."[2]

The eighteenth century saw in the seventeenth century formulation of scientific methods a key to resolving disputes over matters of public interest and making the resolutions public resources. It was an honorable historical development, and scientific methods have continued to exert honorable cultural authority to the present. The same century saw in its continuing exercise of rationality, and in lessons from historical extremes of democracy and despotism, a balanced formula for supervision of public good consistent with individual sovereignty—likewise honorable and authoritative. But as it has happened, matters of public interest are not always scientific or constitutionally affected.

What, then, is to be done when one person's idea of good is someone else's idea of evil? Are these conflicts to be resolved by the natural selection of power gaming or by reasoned persuasion? If by reason, where should reasoned appeal find rest? If by power gaming, what becomes of liberty? To pry civilization off the rational and value-infused platform that only God can supply is to set back knowledge of the right and good and then to set back liberty. The sixth century BC philosopher Epimenides recognized the platform, and the apostle Paul affirmed it, quoting him in the first century, saying, "For in him we live and move and have our being." So said the third century BC poet Aratus as similarly quoted by Paul, "We are his offspring."[3] Perhaps there is a fact here that ought to be more highly valued.

Regardless, life is valued, truth is valued, and liberty is valued. Whether acknowledged or not, this is the evidence, along with the knowledge of good and evil, that the *Imago Dei*—the image of God— is implanted in persons. These values cannot easily be forced out of the public conscience. They shield good and evil from attempts at reinvention. Life, truth, and liberty are charged and drawn into orbit as it were around the knowledge of good and evil. But it is not impossible that power gamers can get in there and by manipulation or redefinition of the nucleus send them flying off in all directions.

Might makes right is ordinary; right makes might is extraordinary. Might makes right is slavery; right makes might is liberty. Petty tyrants and despots have always delighted and will continue to delight in setting up conditions where one must choose to comply with their program or suffer loss—slander, imprisonment, confiscation of property, violent harm, or forcing one to choose between life and liberty, leaving no option to retain both. Nothing suggests that the world has somehow advanced beyond this; that truth is suppressed in unrighteousness[4] is not unusual.

One may arrive, then, at a time when one is forced to decide either to hang on to liberty at the cost of life or let liberty go in exchange for life. Once committed to life, your liberty may soon be gone. Once committed to liberty, your life may soon be gone. Patrick Henry announced his commitment to this second option famously. This is how you know you are free though, when you face opposition. In opposition, faith is distinguished from floating along with the current. Faith can still be free even when truth is not. There are two kinds of religion, then, for those who do not presume to concoct religion: faith-based and fate-based. Faith-based religion is liberty. The image is of truth seekers, once having found it, resolute, upholding it at personal cost. In contrast, fate-based religion is slavery. The image is of noncommittal, self-satisfied skeptics, believing, in cause-effect fashion, whatever is absorbed from the air.

Those who have found their way in through the narrow gate[5] may choose to retain their liberty, knowing that no tyrant or despot can snatch one's life out of the eternal Father's hand.[6] The Father is able to restore life; He cannot restore liberty if you should opt to give that up. Therefore, hang on to liberty. If you are a narrow gate-er, the Almighty has already seen to your preservation and justification. And when they no longer argue against you and they begin trying to kill you, then you know—like Stephen in Acts chapter 7 and many others who have followed in the liberty of faith—that you have prevailed.

Appendix A
Utopian Ideologies

The most notorious utopian societal scheme is named after its chief theorist Karl Heinrich Marx (1818–83). Marxism began as a particularly intractable economic theory—intractable because of its disfigurement of human nature. The disfigurement is the now-discredited idea that economics is the only thing that has ever mattered in history, that everyone is motivated exclusively according to material needs, and that the accumulation of material goods is what produces happiness. On that basis, a collective interest in material equality was made to supersede the individual right to property.

As material enhancements to living began to be churned out by the industrial revolution, the distinction between haves and have-nots, between owners of production and wage-workers, became frightfully acute. In devising a means by which wealth might be more equitably distributed, Marx asserted the right of exploited workers to violently overthrow the owners of property and means of industrial production and claim it for themselves. A collective ownership of all production facilities would then, one would presume, be formed among the workers. Marx's formula was one of a number of reactions against the horrors of the industrial revolution—the deplorable and dangerous conditions inside factories, the squalid conditions of factory towns, and the unconscionable exploitation of factory workers including children. But if Marx gets credit here, he should also get some credit for the far worse horrors that ensued on the Eurasian continent in the next century from Marxist doctrines: the massive famines and death camps of ideological purification; the colossal economic failures and consequent squalor of centralized planning; the social poison of a surveillance state that rewards neighborhood informers; and more in the Soviet Union, communist China, and many other unfortunate countries.

Marxist ideology has all land, natural resources, factories and instruments of production, means of communication and transportation, and credit (that is, banks) owned and controlled by the government, not by individual owners and investors. Marxist ideology posits a "workers' paradise" where, within the framework of collective ownership of the means of production, everyone gives according to their abilities and receives according to their needs—abilities and needs being, of course, determined by the government. Government controls all the benefits of production and commerce and decides who gets what out of the collective. What is not advertised is that the workers' paradise removes motivation for work and for improving the system of production because rewards for work and innovation do not go to those who work and innovate but to the collective. The futility of excellence in productivity and invention was quickly learned. Slacking, apathy, and chronic scarcities of goods were the result. (It is noteworthy that communist China has accepted the failure of Marxist economics in having introduced free market economic practices, though under rigorous supervision.) Yet the redistribution of benefits, as bad as that may be, is not nearly so much the problem. The problem is the fact that someone has to manage it, and that is way too much power for any government.

Marxism is commonly known as communism and has consistently turned out to be a "paradise" from which workers seek to escape. Note that the Berlin Wall was installed to keep people imprisoned in the communist system, not to stop too many from jumping on board. The subtraction of property rights is evil; it means that everyone becomes dependent on the government for their needs. But the confiscatory system does not end with that. Elimination of freedoms of religion, speech, press, the right to assemble peaceably, the right to keep and bear arms, and rights of the accused follows. Marxist revolutionary leaders are aware that the mind really is free and can rise above contentment with material uniformity. To maintain their station, the freedom to think independently of the "benefits" of communism must be suppressed. Government must maintain absolute command over opportunities for the people to challenge its authority. Any tendency for not entirely blissful dependents of the communist scheme to contemplate alternatives to the scheme, and especially to share that contemplation, poses the chief threat to power. Aspirations must be collectivized and aligned to the goals of the state. If any dare to rise above the plain of uniformity, they must be stamped down as out of whack. Uniformity is the ideal on all points. You can see it in the beam of totalitarian communist dictators as their vast armies march before them in perfect unison.

Communism may be forced on a society by terror and violence. *Forced* is indeed the proper term. Communist revolutions have never appeared as initiatives of workers spontaneously rising up and taking over. Revolutions do not happen without leadership, strategic planning, and financing. The intent of communist agitators has never been equitable distribution but rather power through totalitarian control. The population must be divided and set against itself. One segment of the population is persuaded to believe that absolute destruction of another segment—the designated enemy—is a necessity for their well-being. In this, unfortunately, the failure of the economic theory has not eliminated the communist threat to free societies, and today, it exhibits a social as well as economic character. If an identity group can be persuaded to believe themselves oppressed by some other group, they can become a handy tool to stimulate discontent and unrest, same as Marx's wage-worker proletarians. By means of misinformation campaigns that stir up lawless and violent conflict in the streets, a state of agitation, even anarchy, may be produced. Public sympathies may be swayed by underscoring chance actions (even possibly staged actions) by the oppressor group against the oppressed group. Meanwhile, agents of the power grab infiltrate the government and position themselves to appear as those best able to rescue the peace of society when a popular demand arises for government to fix the situation. Marxist strategizers in pockets of academia and the major press and media keep politically correct social and economic equality visions and associated revolutionary possibilities alive and attractive. Inequality is not universally identical to injustice; inequality of property and achievement is not an injustice. Injustice is giving some persons rights against the property and achievements of others without return. But an unaware popular imagination that cannot distinguish between injustice and inequality is vulnerable to the propaganda and seduction of forced programs of "economic and social justice and equality."

Socialism also originated as a reaction to the horrors of the early industrial revolution. It shares the same root as communism having been founded on the same faulty economic principle and misrepresentation of human nature. Same as communism, socialism communalizes and controls economic resources for redistribution. Same as communism, socialism saps the vitality and drive for excellence from persons. Same as communism, the fulfillment of one's needs becomes a bureaucratic function rather than an individual responsibility and source of distinction. Same as communism, uniformity is the ideal. The mass population must be educated continually on the superiority of socialism's collective values. They must be steered clear of ideas about individual rights that run contrary to such values by a blanket of propaganda. Because the prosperity promised by socialism is not what is actually achieved, there is a possibility that some may begin to exhibit discontent. Discontent can be contagious. Thus, same as communism, beliefs and values that supply a foundation for individual rights, such as understood in the Constitution, are fated to fall under condemnation.

Communism eventually separated itself from socialism, taking a more violent revolutionary and international turn. Today, socialism retains a more creeping mode of societal strangulation. But while seeming to distinguish itself from the hard swift edge of communism, socialism's creep only makes it the more insidious. In this contrast, socialism seems often to be driven by a real compassion for the less fortunate. There should be no confusion over this image, however. The compassion that some want to be known for is really only a bid to get the government to do what true compassion does from its own resources. The bid for government to do it, same as communism, is only a measure to gain power.

Among the worst socialist regimes to date was Germany's between 1933 and 1945. Soon after the National Socialist (or Nazi as derived from <u>Na</u>tional So<u>zi</u>alist) German Workers Party attained its rule over the country in 1933, a program of racial ascendency came into view. The ethnic annihilation toward that end was so systematically ghastly and criminal that it is hard to imagine any regime ever following in its steps, though some have gotten close. It was only in degree though and not variation in socialist principle by which such an advanced country went so wrong so quickly and completely. Hard economic times and the appeal of a little strong-armed equalizing of material benefits between native Germans and a certain other more prosperous ethnicity (Jews) mixed with longstanding European anti-Semitism and some coarse propaganda quickly turned into the oppression and then murder of millions of imagined enemies, both within national boundaries and without.[1] This sort of thing can happen, and has happened, again. Beware, then, the signals—propaganda and violence directed against some racial, ethnic, or other group targeted as oppressors, enemies of equality, or holders of incorrect thought.

Two other utopian collectivist ideologies are general political philosophies of more historical and academic interest: utilitarianism and pragmatism. Though no longer in circulation as named, they are still noteworthy in having some attraction that follows a logic similar to Marxism and socialism in their absence of regard for the rights of individuals.

Utilitarianism is the collective pursuit of happiness. A utilitarian policy of law and governance, according to one of its chief proponents, Jeremy Bentham (1748–1832), is that which procures the greatest happiness for the greatest number. Quickly though, the question arises as to how such happiness should be defined and measured. If individual happiness is divergent—what makes one person happy may be not at all what makes another happy—one should not expect a uniform answer to aggregate happiness. Happiness on the individual level may be difficult enough to attain; management of it on an aggregate level might well be an exercise in absurdity. Granting that an after-the-fact measure of happiness might possibly be forthcoming from opinion polls, how one charts a course for future aggregate happiness is the more pertinent matter. Here, the ideal, if not in theory, breaks down in practice: how the greatest happiness for the greatest number is to be interpreted is pretty much up to whoever is able to grab the public's attention and write for it its menu.

Time after time, visions of future economic and social happiness rally great numbers. The shortness of popular collective memory is able to produce a nearly continuous lust for government procured happiness that rushes from one unfulfilled promise to another. But if what causes happiness for one produces unhappiness for another, the utilitarian ideal does break down in theory. There are such conflicts in the public realm, and slavery was at the top of the historical list; there was no possibility that everyone could agree to on what would be the greatest aggregate or collective happiness. In any case, the Declaration of Independence asserts that the pursuit of happiness is an *individual* pursuit, not a collective pursuit. To hand over regulation of happiness to government is too often to encroach upon the right of persons to pursue it on their own terms.

Pragmatism is a particularly American form of collective pursuit originated by Charles Saunders Peirce (1839–1914) and further expounded by William James (1842–1910) and John Dewey (1859– 1952). Here, the value of legislation and governing policy is assessed solely on the practical effects it generates, on whether useful or favorable results are achieved. Similar to utilitarianism, the relevance of higher values and moral concerns to legislation and policy is unrecognized. The inevitable problem is how to judge one set of practical results against an alternate set of practical results. Which pragmatic goals should be pursued? Whose pragmatism should prevail? Pragmatism attempts to evade the admittedly serious difficulties involving higher truth and meaning in a pluralistic society, but in the dilemmas posed by these questions, it runs right up against them. As is the case with utilitarianism, pragmatism is not able to guide resolutions on moral controversies; that is, where one person's idea of good is another's idea of evil. In fact, it has to deny that there are such controversies. Even if slavery and abortion, for example, were justifiable on grounds of practical success, however that success might be ascertained, objections to them are most certainly not. Utilitarian and pragmatic ideals are poor substitutes for recognition of real good and real evil.

Utopian schemes exhibit two operating principles in common: (1) elevate the collective interest over that of the individual and (2) ensure that the definition of the collective interest is reserved to the instigators and maintainers of the utopian scheme. There are no longer citizens with unalienable rights consenting to be governed according to constitutional principles. There are instead only useful factions in the populace whose discontent is leveraged to gain power. Whatever the ideology may be, it serves only as a happy promise to hook the unwary and a platform from which to condemn resistance; it hardly matters in the end.

The prime example is the 1848 Communist Manifesto. The Manifesto was written by Marx, who was commissioned to write it by the Communist League, a group of European intellectuals looking to establish a new nationless world order. It begins, as described above, by economicizing history in such a fashion as to conclude the oppression of the "proletariat" wage-earning working "class" by the self-serving "bourgeois" owners of production facilities as the chief—correction—the sole ill of society. When it finally gets around to introducing the specifics of its revolutionary program to rescue these oppressed toward the end of chapter 2, it is seen to be a program of total government control and absolute destruction of the enemy bourgeois "class." There is no right of property or inheritance (planks 1 and 3). Besides confiscation of land, capital, and the means of production, it calls for absolute control over families and education, elimination of nations and religions, and the reformation of morality to line up with the interests of the state. The state owns the products of labor, not you. It also tells you where you will live (plank 9), what work you will do (plank 8), where you can travel (plank 6), who you can communicate with (plank 6), and what you will think (plank 10). How all this is supposed to free wage-laborers receives no attention whatsoever.

There should be no misunderstanding about the reason for this apparent oversight in the Manifesto. The oppressed class is only a means to stir up discontent, which then provides the pretext for radical, revolutionary upset in the political and social order. Overthrow of the existing political and social order is the objective and totalitarian utopian oppression the end state. The pretext of relief for the oppressed class is not and will be dumped as soon as the discontented have fulfilled their use.

It may be necessary to include democracy in the list of utopian schemes. Democracy is often seen as the ideal form of public decision-making. No doubt, it is often so regarded in America. Whenever decisions are to be made by any private or non-governmental public group, there is near universal assent to democratic means of reaching them. The democratic system is praised as the ultimate in fairness. Granted, the principle of citizen sovereignty would seem, in any practical implementation, necessarily indistinguishable from a democratic process. So why should democracy emit the stench of utopianism?

Democracy may be the worst of political systems (or the worst besides all the others according to Winston Churchill's saying) because it operates on transient whims of the majority. To their credit, at least other ideologies might have some consistency in their possibly having a fixed theory, even while the practicalities of their oppression vary from regime to regime. It was well understood by the authors of the Constitution that democracy produces a tyranny of the majority. They wanted nothing to do with it. "Democracies," wrote the father of the Constitution James Madison (1751–1836) in Federalist 10, "have ever been spectacles of turbulence and contention; have ever been found incompatible with personal security or the rights of property; and have in general been as short in their lives as they have been violent in their deaths."

Madison was well aware from his study of the history of governance in the ancient Mediterranean, as were the other founders, that certain tendencies inevitably arise wherever momentary popular views prevail in government. The tendency is for passion, prejudice, and impulse to prevail over reason, wisdom, and self-control. Without a fixed system of law as in a republic and without a system of representation that distances direct popular control, it is easy to excite the masses to take action over some offense, incident, or condition, real or imagined. Life and personal property are never secure in the presence of an angry mob, and should life and property rights become endangered, so does every other right along with them.

Edmund Burke pinpointed the root problem of democracies in observing that there is nothing to regulate or control the exercise of power by the majority.[2] The people cannot be the control over political power while exercising it. The attraction of pure democracy is undeniable, but its hazard is extreme. The authors of the Constitution wisely charted around the temptation to democratize. The Constitution, as the expression of the people's highest will, elevates their sovereignty while simultaneously keeping it at a distance. Legislative representation moderates momentary democratic zeal while preserving the more enduring sentiments of the people.

How is it possible to resist or contain attempts to create ideal societies? How are persons supposed to detect the subtle ways in which their liberty and rights can be stolen when utopian societal schemes intent on doing just that seem so promising? For many, the temptation to exchange a little freedom for a promise of government-supplied security is irresistible. The answer has to do with the need to persuade a significant mass of people in order to move forward an agenda destructive to liberty. It is not possible to do that when citizens are informed and see a lie for what it is.

Appendix B
Natural Law and Natural Right

There is a considerable history of thought founded on the idea that principles upon which a society should generate its laws may be discovered by consideration of human nature or what it means to be human. The idea may be traced as far back as Aristotle (384–322 BC) in ancient Greece, Marcus Tullius Cicero (106–43 BC) in ancient Rome, and Thomas Aquinas (1224–74) in thirteenth century Western Europe. This school of thought is called natural law theory—the qualifier "natural" referring to human nature, not natural in the sense of physical laws discoverable by science. Natural law theory offers promise that the metaphysical identity problem may be bypassed, tyrannical and arbitrary government thwarted, or both in the search for the proper identifications of what is right, good, and just.

Natural law begins with recognition of a capacity for reasoned deliberation and independent action. This capacity for rationality and autonomy characterizes human beings in contradistinction to every other known thing in the universe. Rationality includes, among other things, the ability to deliberate on and decide what is right and good in any specific circumstance. Autonomy or freedom of will is the independence from causal factors, both natural and supernatural, to act upon such decisions. The success of natural law theory is measured by what boundaries it is able to codify for all humanity—that is, what laws it has found to be objective and universal. Natural law theory recognizes that civilizations and cultures vary in their laws. But it also presupposes that the roots of difference do not extend below all rationality such that it is impossible to find at least some common ground upon which to devise just legal systems. What side of the road one must drive on may be a matter of convention, but laws against murder and theft, it may be asserted, are objective and universal.

Relations between individuals and between individuals and society appeal to the principle of reciprocity. By way of example, that each person seeks self-preservation is understood, and by reciprocity, laws against murder are a consequence. If I respect your life, you are required to return the same respect to mine. That each person is in command of their property is understood, and by reciprocity, no one may appropriate it without permission just as that person, in reciprocity, should not do so to someone else's. Laws against theft are thereby established by reciprocity as universal. Reciprocity is encapsulated by the golden rule (Do unto others as you would have them do unto you) or the silver rule (Do not do unto others what you would not have them do unto you). The contribution of natural law theory is in basing laws on something more certain than what a governing authority or what a majority of citizens in their legislations may happen to find expedient or popular at any given time. The principle of reciprocity supplies natural law theory with the essence of that something.

Perhaps the most straightforward way to think about natural law and perhaps its chief contribution is the recognition that some laws are unjust. The Constitution's circumspections toward slavery prior to ratification of the Thirteenth Amendment, for example, were seen to be inconsistent with the rights of liberty and the pursuit of happiness and, therefore, unjust. This was particularly the case with Constitution's provision for the return of fugitive slaves in Article IV, Section 2, a provision that was defied by many for precisely that reason, as unjust. How does one distinguish between just and unjust laws? The governing authority cannot just tack up some laws on the bulletin board and expect them to be honored solely because they are there. There is more to law than arbitrarily throwing some rules out there because everyone likes to obey rules. They do not. Natural law theory asserts that there is a higher law than legislated law—law that stirs conscience and by which legislated law may be judged as worthy or unworthy, as just or unjust. As much as higher law is often intuitive and ill-defined, that higher law, if and once it can be defined and rationally defended, is what natural law is. There is more to rightness, goodness, and justice than service to a set of legal procedures for enacting laws and for judging cases under those laws. Failure of legislation and courts of law to heed this point diminishes respect for them.

Associated with natural law are natural rights. English philosopher John Locke (1632–1704) in the 1689 *Second Treatise of Government* first recognized rights of life, liberty, and property, which the Declaration of Independence and the Fifth and Fourteenth amendments to the Constitution draw upon. Similar to natural law, natural rights also proceed from rationality, autonomy, and reciprocity. Natural right is the freedom to exercise one's rationality and autonomy in the determination of ends or goals and the means to pursue them. Rationality and autonomy are inextricably linked to the choosing of ends and their means, ends and means that may be compared as to their rightness and goodness. Each person's ends and means are at their disposition. The presumption of reciprocity is that each person having a fully developed rationality is as much able and responsible for determining his or her own ends and means as anyone else. If there is equality in the determination, then there must exist equality in the freedom to pursue as well.

There are limits to this freedom. The obligation imposed by reciprocity is in not over-exercising one's right to ends and means to the detriment of the reciprocal right of someone else. A right cannot be at the expense of another or the larger society. Normally, this is not a problem. The right to one's own life does not generally nullify the reciprocal claim of another; the right to one's own property does not often subtract from the same claim by others to their property. The right to choose a religion or belief system does not usually compromise another's right to likewise choose a religion or belief system. It is seldom the case that reciprocal obligations might not be honored in principle. But acceptance of the principle does not always lead to its practice and reciprocity is not universally observed. The right to defend one's rights, or the right of self-defense, even though fundamental to all other rights, does not itself secure a state of liberty if one is forced into continual preoccupation with such defense. Therefore, an administration of justice must mark and enforce the boundaries against over-exercise of rights. The securing of individual rights is, as Locke first asserted and as the Declaration of Independence affirms, a government's sole responsibility.

There is a need for consent to taxation to serve the natural rights of all, in particular, to maintain administrations of justice and armed forces that might also require compulsory jury duty or military service. Those needs are limited. Beyond them, freedom from compulsory demands may apply. Natural right is also reminiscent of the golden rule. The basis of natural right in reciprocity was well stated by German philosopher Immanuel Kant (1724–1804) when he wrote on freedom as a fundamental right:

> Freedom is independence of the compulsory will of another; and in so far as it can coexist with the freedom of all according to a universal law, it is the one sole original, inborn right belonging to every man in virtue of his humanity. There is, indeed, an innate equality belonging to every man which consists in his right to be independent of being bound by others to anything more than that to which he may also reciprocally bind them.[1]

Nevertheless, even as natural law and natural right have a well-established theory, in practice, that is, in the determination of actual laws and rights, success has been less than universal. Some matters such as land, water, and air rights, the right to appeal for economic aid from government, and the right of foreigners to immigrate can only be run through the political process. In other matters, rights that were once obvious become unsettled because of the effect of changing conceptions of reality on the social order. An example is the debate over the right to keep and bear arms. The appalling and senseless massacres in public schools and other public places by a few deranged individuals leave some to think that there is no alternative to stop the mayhem than to tighten control over ownership of firearms. On the other side is the long-established right acknowledged by the Second Amendment by which free people may not only defend themselves against these and other malcontents but also maintain a deterrent against an overzealous government contemplating the advantages of tyranny in solving many problems. Guns have been around for a long time and so have public schools and public places. But this problem is much more recent. It would seem that there is a root cause lurking below the level of popular awareness that is not called up. The effect of some taking false though common conceptions of reality too seriously is not being debated. So contention and irresolution persist.

Natural law and natural right have not always been regarded favorably and have even been opposed in principle. Many other influential philosophers over the last few centuries—Thomas Hobbes, David Hume, Jean Jacques Rousseau, Jeremy Bentham, John Stuart Mill, William James, John Dewey, and others—have attempted to stand natural law theory on its head. They have refused the earlier confidence that laws and rights may be objective and universal and have generally prevailed. They have introduced the idea that laws have no basis other than social agreement or a "social contract." Moral psychologist Jonathan Haidt poses a question as to the existence of natural rights in such a manner as to make the idea seem ridiculous— that if they exist, they have to be comparable to "mathematical truths sitting on a cosmic shelf next to the Pythagorean theorem just waiting to be discovered by Platonic reasoners."[2] The idea is that laws and rights are invented, not discovered.

Little importance is attached to natural law and natural right in the conception of democratic liberty today. It is a consequence of the erosion of the idea of creation and a fixed human nature. The nature of human nature has become elusive, and laws and rights are no longer accommodated to a human nature that is inherent and able to be deduced. Rather, they are declared and open to revision as legislatures and judiciaries with a legislative bent see fit and which is more and more on the ground of political expediency.[3,4]

Therefore, however much natural law and natural right may be, or may have once been reasoned from rationality, autonomy, and reciprocity, one cannot entirely disassociate them from a metaphysical basis and expect them to remain unassaulted. Notably, the Declaration of Independence cuts short such reasoning and straightforwardly asserts that rights are Creator-based, which, in view of the inability of natural causes to account for rationality and autonomy of will as well as the sense of rightness, goodness, and justice, is where they belong anyway.

Appendix C
To What May Be Attributed the Increase and Expansion of Christianity?

Having been sustained for so many centuries as a government tool, at least in part, of public order, oppression, conquest, etc., how Christianity ever got so much traction in the ancient world of Rome may be fairly questioned. Historians have not overlooked the causes of such an important transformation in world history as the conversion of the ancient empire from paganism to Christianity. However, it appears that there are few sources enabling the historian to piece together the causes of Christianity's increase and expansion prior to the fourth century, which is when the government took over responsibility for that. The lack of sources is evident in even the most recent works on the subject.[1] Thus, historians are forced to draw on, in their own judgment, a biased religious source, the New Testament, and in particular the New Testament book *The Acts of the Apostles*. Because of its "religious" nature and "bias," the cautionary use historians make of Acts is regulated by how such use is likely to be viewed by their academic peers. At least some of its content is, therefore, dismissed as non-historical, especially the reports of miracles.

While historians speculate over the matter, the circumstances of the first century and the New Testament book of Acts do make clear what produced converts. Christianity was not a religious inheritance according to family ancestry, tribal association, or ethnicity, nor was it delineated by territory, geographic vicinity, or political jurisdiction until centuries later. It was not imposed by imperial decree or military conquest until centuries later. Christianity was widely denounced, poorly esteemed, and of uncertain and variable legal status in its first few centuries. Everywhere it was spoken against.[2] Time after time, the Jewish chief priests, Pharisees and scribes, and other Jews resorted to coercive pressures including execution to extinguish the movement.[3] They were equaled and replaced in this soon after by Roman governing authorities in sporadic harassments until legalization upon the ascension of Constantine to the emperorship in AD 312 and toleration under the Edict of Milan in AD 313. From the record of the book of Acts, how the Apostles drew converts by reasoned argument from the Old Testament is understood. It was not necessarily always an appetite for belief in miracles:

> Acts 2:14–42—Peter addresses the crowd at Pentecost of which approximately 3,000 were persuaded by his arguments, in part, appealing to the Old Testament and quoting from the prophet Joel and from Psalms 16 and 110.
>
> Acts 3:12–26—Peter again addresses a crowd in the temple, appealing to his listeners' knowledge of the Old Testament and how the prophets had foretold the recent events concerning Jesus.
>
> Acts 4:8–12—Peter and John are confronted by the Jewish high council for teaching about the resurrection of the Lord Jesus and reference Psalm 118:22 in defense.
>
> Acts 7:1–53—Stephen answers his accusers before the council by recounting a large swath of Old Testament history which then becomes the basis for his turning back their accusations about his departure from the law of Moses and the temple back on themselves.
>
> Acts 8:26–37—Philip explains the significance of Isaiah chapter 53 to the events surrounding Jesus's ministry to an Ethiopian official.
>
> Acts 9:20–22—Paul confounds Jews in Damascus by proving that Jesus was the Christ, which can be done only

by reference to the Old Testament because no concept of a Christ (Messiah) existed apart from it.

Acts 10:43—Peter makes mention of the witness of the prophets in establishing forgiveness of sins in the name of the Savior, Jesus.

Acts 13:16–41—Paul, in the synagogue at Antioch, presents a case for Jesus being the promised Savior and his resurrection from the dead by appealing to his hearers' knowledge of the Old Testament and quoting from Psalms and the prophet Habakkuk.

Acts 15:13–21—James appeals to the prophet Amos, decisively resolving a controversy over the admission of Gentile converts into the church, on whether they first needed to convert to Judaism.

Acts 17:2–4—Paul, in the synagogue at Thessalonica, reasons from the scriptures, as was his custom, explaining and proving that is was necessary for the Christ to suffer and rise from dead, and saying "This Jesus, whom I proclaim to you, is the Christ."

Acts 17:11—The Bereans, in order to verify the things being taught by Paul, search the Old Testament scriptures.

Acts 18:4–5—Paul, at Corinth, reasons in the synagogue, "testifying to the Jews that the Christ was Jesus."

Acts 18:24–28—Apollos, at Corinth, confutes the Jews in public, "showing by the scriptures that the Christ was Jesus."

Acts 19:8—Paul, at Ephesus, argues in the synagogue on behalf of the kingdom of God, and being opposed, goes next door to the Hall of Tyrannus and argues daily for a period of approximately two years.

Acts 26:22–23,27—Paul, stressing that he makes no claim but what was spoken by the prophets and Moses, appeals to King Agrippa's belief in the prophets.

Acts 28:23–24—Paul, to a Jewish audience, and while under house arrest at Rome, expounds and testifies to the kingdom of God and to Jesus from the law of Moses and the prophets.

During this time, there were competing claims to truth and authority, the Jews, Rome, and the apostles. It was easy to spot which was likely to be authentic and which was not. Truth suppressers invariably back up their claim to authority with misrepresentations or threats and unjust encroachments against person, property, or mobility. Truth upholders back theirs with reasoned appeal. Reasoned appeal may not always guarantee the presence of truth, but it does at least suggest the possibility of it, especially when its representatives persist through violent opposition. In this case, the presence of truth was guaranteed by the convergence of numerous and diverse forward-looking Old Testament lines, each of which had originated in distinct historical settings. The first century convergence of these prophetic lines remains the focal point of history, even as academics try to make BC (Before Christ) become BCE (Before Common Era) and replace AD (Ano Domini or the year of our Lord) with CE (Common Era). Nevertheless, one may still ask, "What makes the era common?" It appears that some people were interested in truth, even if it was going to cost them.

Soon after Constantine's ascension in the early fourth century, Christianity was Romanized—meaning centralized in administration under the emperor's custodianship. It also became a recipient of government favor and financing. In the late fourth century under the emperor Theodosius I, Christianity was declared the official religion of the empire. Thereafter, reasoned persuasion became unnecessary. When government upholds and provides for the religion, the religion has little need for other means to assure its acceptance and continuity. The financial sustenance and administrative unity provided by Constantine and his successors also made the church an avenue of opportunistic upward mobility, furthering the attraction of membership.[4] Reasoned arguments of the sort advanced in the first century have largely been out of use since. Even more, fragmentation of religious authority and doctrines in the sixteenth century and consequent wars of religion rather seemed to exhaust the expectation that truth in matters of religion could be attained. Certainly, war was a total breakdown in the manner in which Christianity was supposed to be propagated.

Now that in the United States, government is more out of the business of religion than ever before, it is again reasoned and perhaps impassioned persuasion that must assure acceptance and continuity. However, the reasoned persuasion on offer today seems less than many challenges against it demand. In view of their disuse, it is not clear whether the arguments advanced by the apostles in the first century can regain their effectiveness.

Notes

Chapter 1: Liberty

1. Edmund Burke, "Speech on Moving His Resolutions for Conciliation with the Colonies," March 22, 1775, *Edmund Burke: Reflections on the Revolution in France and Other Writings*, p. 170. Edmund Burke (1729– 97), a British statesman sympathetic to the American cause, here describes the American mindset just prior to the Revolution.
2. The constitutional principle of separate legislative, executive, and judicial branches had been formalized by French political philosopher Charles-Louis de Second at Baron de La Brede et de Montesquieu (1689–1755) in the 1748 work *Spirit of the Laws*. Montesquieu expounded upon this three-fold separation of governmental powers, recognizing the despotic dangers of their combination under one head. Montesquieu's vision of republican government in *Spirit of the Laws* was widely referenced and debated during the American founding era.
3. Principles embedded in the Magna Carta included independence of the church from the king, prohibition of punitive taxation, no taxation without representation, consent of the governed, trial by jury of peers, the right to a speedy trial, the writ of habeas corpus or the requirement to have evidence presented upon an accusation of crime, punishments appropriate to the crimes, and prohibition of purchased justice, that is, uniform justice for everyone regardless of their economic means.

4. The placing of government and governed under the same law was not a new idea. Deuteronomy 17:18–20 shows that kings in ancient Israel were particularly called out to make certain that they kept the same laws that everyone else was under—in that case, the laws of God. They were not to elevate themselves above the laws or the people. "And when he sits on the throne of his kingdom, he shall write for himself in a book a copy of this law, from that which is in charge of the Levitical priests, and it shall be with him, and he shall read in it all the days of his life, that he may learn to fear the LORD his God, by keeping all the words of this law and these statutes, and doing them; that his heart may not be lifted up above his brethren, and that he may not turn aside from the commandment, either to the right hand or to the left; so that he may continue long in his kingdom, he and his children, in Israel" (RSV).

5. Whether proprietary (commercial) or crown (royal), the charter of each colony contained specifications on how it was to be administered. Included in these charters were compilations of liberties and privileges understood as originating in English law and custom. The charters prefigured written constitutions and bills of rights. (See Bernard Bailyn, pp. 190–198.) The executive, judicial, and legislative functions of government were largely in the hands of colonists, not the English government, as the following statements indicate: "Despite the efforts that had been made by the English government in the late seventeenth century to reduce the areas of local jurisdiction in the colonies, local provincial autonomy continued to characterize American life… It had, in fact, been local, common law courts that administered justice in the colonies; the courts associated with the home government [England] had been condemned as 'prerogative,' their jurisdiction repeatedly challenged and closely restricted… The power of taxing, from the earliest years of settlement, had been exercised by the representative assemblies of the various

colonies, and exercised without competition—indeed with encouragement—from England." (See Bailyn, pp. 203–204.) The absence of the government of England's oversight of the colonies' internal affairs during the colonial period meant that the colonies were self-governing by default. Each colony formed an assembly of elected representatives to decide and enforce policy on matters of public interest, including taxation and the protection of property. By the time of the revolution, American colonists were long accustomed to and experienced with self-government. The above quotations from THE IDEOLOGICAL ORIGINS OF THE AMERICAN REVOLUTION by Bernard Bailyn appear by permission of the publisher: The Belknap Press of Harvard University Press, Cambridge, Mass., Copyright ©1967, 1992 by the President and Fellows of Harvard College.

6. This constitutional principle of consent and sovereignty had been set forth by English philosopher John Locke (1632–1704) in 1690 as an extension of the assertion of parliamentary authority over the king in England's Glorious Revolution of 1688. Here, nearly a century prior to the American founding era, Locke's *Second Treatice of Government* began a political theory built on the platform that the sole duty of government was to uphold the natural rights of individuals and identifying natural rights of life, liberty, and property. The 1690 essay was subtitled *An Essay Concerning the True Original Extent and End of Civil Government*. Rights were natural in the sense that they are inherent to individuals by virtue of their humanity, not grants by government. Locke further theorized that government was legitimate only when it operated under the voluntary consent of the governed. Along with Montesquieu, Locke was one of the most influential authors in the thinking of the founding generation in America.

7. Bernard Bailyn, *The Ideological Origins of the American Revolution*, pp. 95–98, 255–257. Note: Separatists were

religious groups who urged separation from the established church of England as opposed to Puritans who urged purification (reform) of the established church.
8. Edmund Burke, observing the trajectory of the French Revolution, wrote "The spirit of their rule is exactly correspondent to the means by which they obtained it," "Letter to a Member of the National Assembly [France] in Answer to Some Objections to His Book on French Affairs," January 19, 1791, *Edmund Burke, Reflections on the Revolution in France and Other Writings*, p. 680.
9. Thomas Jefferson, primary author of the Declaration, wrote subsequently: "When forced, therefore, to resort to arms for redress, an appeal to the tribunal of the world was deemed proper for our justification," May 8, 1825 Letter to Henry Lee, *Thomas Jefferson, Writings*, p. 1501.

Chapter 2: Debates—Lincoln vs. Douglas

1. Allan C. Guelzo, *Lincoln and Douglas: The Debates That Defined America*, p. 262.
2. Bernard Bailyn, *The Ideological Origins of the American Revolution*, p. 236.
3. Excerpt from "Republican Party Platform of 1856," *The U.S. Constitution: A Reader*, pp. 481–482.
4. Lewis E. Lehrman, *Lincoln at Peoria*, p. 181; Allan C. Guelzo, *Lincoln and Douglas*, pp. 99–104.
5. *Amendment XIV: Equal Protection*, pp. 26–27, 54–55; *Amendment XIV: Due Process*, p. 49.
6. Rodney Stark, *How the West Won*, pp. 119–126, 229–232; *The Victory of Reason*, pp. 23–31, 76–78, 200–202, 220. Stark here argues that the conception of moral equality drawn from Christianity was the chief factor in both instances.
7. The New Testament, in particular, views the moral standing of king as no higher than slave and slave as no lesser than king. In Galatians 3:28, the status of all converts

to Christianity is seen to be the same whether they were Jew, Greek, slave, free, male, or female. Slaves and their masters had the same moral standing, and the command to do good was as much on slaves as on masters in Ephesians 6:5–8. The very fact that salvation was as much available to slaves as it was to masters confirms this point about equality. All those in Christ are declared equal in the eyes of the Almighty, and there is no partiality as seen in Acts 10:34–35, Ephesians 6:9, and James 2:1–7. The Old Testament, while not prohibiting slavery, did set limits on its duration and severity (see Exodus 21:2, Leviticus 25:39–55, Deuteronomy 15:12-15, 18, and Jeremiah 34:8–20). It could also be voluntary as in Exodus 21:5-6 and Deuteronomy 15:16-17. The elimination of slavery is not made an issue in the New Testament; owners were not commanded to free their slaves, so owning slaves was not a sin. Nevertheless, the logical consequence of the biblical principle of moral equality makes the continuation of slavery a contradiction; no one should exist to be an instrument of another.

Federalist vs. Anti-Federalist

8. Thomas L Pangle, *The Great Debate: Advocates and Opponents of the American Constitution*, Lecture 3.
9. Ibid.
10. Ibid, Lecture 2.
11. Ibid, Lecture 4.
12. Ibid.
13. The republican form of government is the rule of law as contrasted to democracy which is the rule of the majority. The difference can be subtle because majority opinion is operative in both forms. The difference arises from the republican form being government under limitations, specified functions, and set procedures that it is not at liberty to modify—in the present case, as stipulated in

the Constitution. In contrast to democracy with its direct polling of citizens for decisions on matters of public interest, popular opinion in a republic may also be moderated through forms of citizen representation instead of direct participation.
14. Pangle, Lecture 6.

Federalist vs. Anti-Federalist II: Judicial Review

15. Thomas L. Pangle, *The Great Debate: Advocates and Opponents of the American Constitution*, Lecture 11.
16. Ibid.
17. Ibid.
18. "June 12, 1823, Letter to Justice William Johnson," *Thomas Jefferson, Writings*, p. 1475, and "September 7, 1803, Letter to Wilson Cary Nicholas," p. 1140.

Chapter 3: The Wall

1. The national anthem affirms this point in its fourth verse: "Oh thus be it ever when free men shall stand, between their loved homes and the war's desolation; Blessed with victory and peace, *may the heaven rescued land, praise the power that hath made and preserved us a nation*; Then conquer we must, when our cause it is just, *and this be our motto 'In God is our trust;*' And the Star-Spangled Banner in triumph shall wave, o'er the land of the free, and the home of the brave" (emphasis added).
2. "May 8, 1825, Letter to Henry Lee," *Thomas Jefferson, Writings*, p. 1501: "Neither aiming at originality of principle or sentiment, nor yet copied from any particular and previous writing, it was intended to be an expression of the American mind, and to give to that expression the proper tone and spirit called for by the occasion. All its

authority rests then on the harmonizing sentiments of the day."
3. Patrick Henry introduced a bill to the Virginia legislature in late 1784 titled "A Bill Establishing a Provision for Teachers of the Christian Religion." The bill did not establish a state denomination. It allowed the taxpayer to designate a denomination to receive the tax. Nevertheless, the tax would be obligatory. James Madison's arguments against the proposal are contained in *Memorial and Remonstrance*.
4. "Memorial and Remonstrance Against Religious Assessments," *James Madison, Writings*, pp. 29–36.
5. The separation between church and state was not a new idea. The Old Testament had a secure concept of the separation between church and state in its separation between priest and king. In ancient Israel, the king could not be a priest, and a priest could not be the king. The religious authority and the authority of state were in separate hands. The separation of religious and governing authority did not mean, however, that the role of religion in cultivating public virtue would be prevented.
6. *Metaphysics* is a term originating from the ancient Greek philosopher Aristotle and refers to the study of that which may exist beyond the physical or natural world or beyond what may be perceived by the senses (i.e., transcendent, spiritual, or supernatural). Metaphysics is also the branch of philosophy that deals with what reality there may be beyond or behind physical reality.
7. A description of the historical development of secularization, pluralization, and privatization in Western civilization may be found in Part I of Ravi Zacharias's, *Deliver Us from Evil*, pp. 3–117.
8. Judges 17:6 and 21:25.
9. The Islamic religion appeared in the early seventh century and was quickly propagated by military aggression and forced conversion of peoples in the Middle East, North Africa, and Central and Southeast Asia. In contrast to

Christianity, the immediacy of the Islamic conquests cannot easily be construed as the result of a religion commandeered by an agenda having nothing to do with its founding principles. Aggression and oppression are inherent properties of Islam and lurk behind its religious terms *jihad* and *sharia* respectively. Fortunately, people do not, in general, perpetuate a state of aggression unless driven to it politically, and the vast majority of Muslims are peaceful and respectful. It seems possible to stress the moral uprightness and spirituality associated with religion in general. But there should be no illusion that coercion and geopolitical goals are absent from its character. Islamism is an insistent ideology, and Islamic states resemble Marxist states in their intolerance for public criticism and alternate religious perspectives.

10. C.S. Lewis, "The Poison of Subjectivism," *Christian Reflections*, p. 81.
11. Publicly owned land was available to be claimed by settlement until the Taylor Grazing Act of 1934 ended that means of disposition into private ownership.
12. Edmund Burke, "Letter to a Member of the National Assembly," January 19, 1791, *Edmund Burke, Reflections on the Revolution in France and Other Writings*, p. 680.
13. Alexis de Tocqueville, Hugh Brogan, *Alexis de Tocqueville*, p. 320.
14. Oz Guinness, *A Free People's Suicide*, pp. 99–129.
15. Benjamin Franklin, April 17, 1787, *America's God and Country Encyclopedia of Quotations*, p. 247.
16. Benjamin Rush, "Essays, Literary, Moral and Philosophical," 1798, (Thomas and William Bradford, Philadelphia, 1806), p. 8; *America's Founding Fathers*, p. 202.
17. John Adams, "Address to the Military," October 11, 1798, *America's God and Country Encyclopedia of Quotations*, pp. 10–11.
18. James Madison, "Speech in the Virginia Ratifying Convention on the Judicial Power," June 20, 1788, *James Madison, Writings*, p. 398.

19. Samuel Adams, Essay appearing in "The Public Adviser," 1749, *America's God and Country Encyclopedia of Quotations*, p. 23.
20. Alexander Hamilton, "The Stand," April 7, 1798, *The Works of Alexander Hamilton*, Henry Cabot Lodge, ed., Volume VI, (New York: G. P. Putnam, 1904), p. 277.
21. Tyron Edwards, ed., *A Dictionary of Thoughts: Being A Cyclopedia of Laconic Quotations from the Best Authors of the World, Both Ancient and Modern*, (Detroit: F. B. Dickerson Co., 1908), p. 300.
22. Jonathan Haidt, *The Righteous Mind*, pp. 53–56, 220.
23. Ibid. In Part I, Haidt presents empirical evidence that intuition rules people's moral judgments, and that if reasoning is applied, it is only for after-the-fact justification of moral intuitions. The subjects of his investigations rarely questioned the rightness of their intuition. Among the conclusions drawn were these: "We do moral reasoning not to reconstruct the actual reasons why *we ourselves* came to a judgment; we reason to find the best possible reasons *why somebody else ought to join us* in our judgment" (p. 52); "You'll misunderstand moral reasoning if you think about it as something people do by themselves in order to figure out the truth" (p. 59); "If you ask people to believe something that violates their intuitions, they will devote their efforts to finding an escape hatch—a reason to doubt your argument or conclusion. They will almost always succeed" (p. 59). The above quotations are reprinted with permission.
24. Bertrand Russell, *A History of Western Philosophy*, (New York: Simon & Schuster, 1945, 1972), p. xxiii.
25. John Stuart Mill quoted in Gertrude Himmelfarb, *The Moral Imagination*, pp. 106–107.

Chapter 4: Truth, That Which Corresponds to Reality

1. John Locke as referenced in R.C. Sproul's *The Consequences of Ideas*, p. 97.

2. C.S. Lewis, *Miracles*, p. 2. MIRACLES by CS Lewis © copyright CS Lewis Pte Ltd. 1947, 1960. Reprinted with permission.
3. This does not mean that one cannot appeal to nature to ascertain the existence of a creator. It only means that arguing from nature is not effective with those who are already predisposed against arguments from nature. Romans 1:20 says that the nature of God is evident from creation. The full-blown philosophy of evolutionism did not exist when the letter of Paul to the Romans was written. The mind fashioned in the image of God, however, is within the scope of creation.
4. Rodney Stark, *How the West Won*, p. 163.
5. The following is quoted from philosopher and mathematician Alfred North Whitehead's *Science and the Modern World* in support of this point: "But for science, something more is wanted than a general sense of the order in things. It needs but a sentence to point out how the habit of definite exact thought was implanted in the European mind by the long dominance of scholastic logic and scholastic divinity. The habit remained after the philosophy [scholasticism] had been repudiated, the priceless habit of looking for an exact point and sticking to it when found... I do not think, however, that I have even yet brought out the greatest contribution of medievalism to the formation of the scientific movement. I mean the inexpugnable belief that every detailed occurrence can be correlated with its antecedents in a perfectly definite manner, exemplifying general principles. Without this belief, the incredible labours of scientists would be without hope. It is this instinctive conviction, vividly poised before the imagination, which is the motive power of research—that there is a secret, a secret which can be unveiled. . . When we compare this tone of thought in Europe with the attitude of other civilizations when left to themselves, there seems but one source for its origin. It must come

from the medieval insistence on the rationality of God, conceived as with the personal energy of Jehovah and with the rationality of a Greek philosopher. Every detail was supervised and ordered: the search into nature could only result in the vindication of the faith in rationality... In Asia, the conceptions of God were of a being who was either too arbitrary or too impersonal for such ideas to have much effect on instinctive habits of mind. Any definite occurrence might be due to the fiat of an irrational despot, or might issue from some impersonal, inscrutable origin of things... My explanation is that the faith in the possibility of science, generated antecedently to the development of modern scientific theory, is an unconscious derivative from medieval theology." From *Science and the Modern World* by Alfred North Whitehead, pp. 17–18. Copyright © 1925 by The Macmillan Company. Copyright renewed © 1953 by Evelyn Whitehead. Reprinted with permission of The Free Press, a division of Simon & Schuster Children's Publishing Division. All rights reserved.

6. It should be noted that science must continuously strive against a logical fallacy called *the fallacy of affirming the consequent*. The fallacy has to do with the logic of hypotheses. Hypotheses take the form of if-then syllogisms. If a hypothesis is true, then certain results should follow. However, even if they do follow, that does not prove the hypothesis true because factors other than those hypothesized may be partly or wholly responsible for producing the results. Much of the work of the scientist involves the design of experiments that eliminate as many non-hypothesized causal factors as possible.

7. C.S. Lewis, *Miracles*, pp. 17–36. In the chapter titled "The Cardinal Difficulty of Naturalism," Lewis presents an argument against naturalism based on this distinction between cause and effect and rational inference.

8. Alan Sokal, *Beyond the Hoax*, pp. 106–107.

9. Nancy Pearcey, *Saving Leonardo*, pp. 237–238.

10. R.C. Sproul, *The Consequences of Ideas*, pp. 41–42.
11. All one needs to do to verify this fragmentation is to view the art or listen to the music that reflects the latest intellectual trends. Nancy Pearcey tracks the linkage between intellectual trends and art through history in *Saving Leonardo*.
12. Philosophy contains three general categories of inquiry: (1) ontology (what may exist beyond the reach of sensory perception or what is ultimately real) and epistemology (how such knowledge may be attained and made certain); (2) conduct (ethics and morality or how one should live); and (3) governance (law and political organization or how people may best be governed). It is generally advisable that the problem of conduct be answered in view of the conclusions of ontology and epistemology and that the problem of governance is settled in view of the findings regarding conduct.
13. C.S. Lewis, *Mere Christianity*, pp. 3–32.
14. Romans 2:1–3 aptly describes this phenomenon.
15. Genesis 4:9, RSV.
16. Luke 13:14–17, RSV.
17. Matthew 26:69–75, 27:3–5.
18. Jeremiah 17:9, RSV.
19. John 1:23, RSV.
20. Beware of what is termed the Euthyphro dilemma: Is God constrained by moral coordinates, or does God invent moral coordinates arbitrarily? It is a false dilemma. Moral coordinates do not rule over God nor does God invent them arbitrarily. There is a third possibility that goodness proceeds from the nature and character of God. The Euthyphro dilemma dates from Plato's dialog *Euthyphro* wherein Socrates asks Euthyphro, "Is the pious loved by the gods because it is pious, or is it pious because it is loved by the gods?"
21. Mark 4:23, NIV.
22. Exodus 3:14, RSV.

23. Exodus 32:8, RSV.
24. Isaiah 6:11 RSV.
25. See Jeremiah 12:1–6, 15:10–12 and 15–18, 20:1–18, 26:1–15, 37:1–15, and 38:1–6.
26. See 1 Kings 22:5–6, Jeremiah 23:13–17, 21–22, 25–27, 30–32, and 37:19, and Ezekiel 13:1–16.
27. The Old Testament passages that promise restoration and deliverance are too numerous to list here exhaustively. Examples may be found in Psalm 2, Psalm 89:19–37, Psalm 110, Isaiah 54, 60–62, Jeremiah 30–31, Amos 9:11–15, Micah 7:8–20, and Zephaniah 3:8–20.
28. See Acts 15:1–21.
29. An introduction to specific Old Testament prophecies and their New Testament fulfillment may be found in Jay Wilson's *Proof That the Bible Is the Word of God* sections titled "Fulfilled Messianic Prophecy" and "The Plan," (http://www.newcreationstudies.org/newcreation/proof.htm).
30. 1 Corinthians 15:3–4.
31. Acts 17:2–3, RSV.
32. See Acts 13:14–15 and 27, and 15:21.
33. Matthew 11:4–5.

Chapter 5: Freedom in a Godless World

1. Proverbs 18:17, NIV.
2. Philip Kitcher, *Life After Faith*, pp. 34–35.
3. Jonathan Haidt, *The Righteous Mind*, pp. 296–313.
4. Ibid, pp. 53–56, 86. The findings are certainly true, but it does not follow that reason "was designed to seek justification, not truth." Note that philosopher David Hume goes so far as to state, "Reason is, and ought only to be the slave of the passions, and can never pretend to any other office than to serve and obey them." Hume, *A Treatise of Human Nature*, p. 462.

5. The 2014 United States Supreme Court case *Burwell v. Hobby Lobby*. The Court's decision aligned with the First Amendment's Free Exercise Clause but only by a 5-4 vote.
6. Erwin W. Lutzer, *When a Nation Forgets God*, pp. 82–88.
7. Malachi 4:6.
8. Romans 1:24–32 describes the trend toward degradation.
9. The Brown case was decided under the Fourteenth Amendment's Equal Protection Clause. Segregation might have been constitutional as was decided in an earlier 1896 case, *Plessy v. Ferguson*. In practice, however, separate but equal was never equal, and it was about time to give up on that delusion.

Chapter 6: Liberty Revisited

1. See for example John 8:31–32, Romans 8:21, 2 Corinthians 3:17, Galatians 5:1, and Hebrews 2:14–15.
2. Matthew 6:10, RSV.
3. Luke 13:23–24, RSV.
4. Daniel N. Robinson, *The Great Ideas of Philosophy, 2nd Edition*, Lecture 32.
5. Genesis 3:1, NIV.
6. The principle is seen in Philemon 8–9: "Accordingly, though I am bold enough in Christ to command you to do what is required, yet for love's sake I prefer to appeal to you" (RSV).
7. Genesis 3:5, RSV.
8. See Genesis 3:5, 22, Isaiah 14:12–14, and Ezekiel 28:2–17.
9. See Genesis 2:17 and 3:19.
10. See Hebrews 2:15.
11. Luke 4:5–7, John 12:31, 14:30, Ephesians 6:11–12, 1 John 5:19.
12. Again, the condition is noted in Romans 2:1–3.
13. John 9:33, RSV.
14. Psalms 115:3, RSV.
15. John 18:38, RSV.

16. Deuteronomy 5:22, RSV.
17. John 18:36, "My kingship is not of this world" (RSV). See also Luke 4:5–8 and John 6:15.
18. It is common for Christianity to be denounced because of evils done in the name of Christianity in past centuries (state-enforced religion, inquisitions and witch trials, the crusades and religiously motivated wars, and imperialism and colonialism). It is true that evils have been done in the name of Christianity. But what has thus been passed off as Christianity must be dismissed as Christianity if inconsistent with its founding principles.

Chapter 7: Writing on the Wall

1. *Everson v. Board of Education*, 1947.
2. Acts 17:27, KJV.
3. Acts 17:28, NIV. The sources are identified in the NIV study note, *Zondervan NIV Study Bible* (Grand Rapids: Zondervan, 2002).
4. Romans 1:18.
5. Matthew 7:13–14 and Luke 13:24.
6. John 10:27–29. See also Hebrews 2:14–15.

Appendix A: Utopian Ideologies

1. The racial utopian ideology of Nazi-ism is often given the label of fascism. Fascism appeared in 1920s Italy, and Italian and other contemporary governments loosely labeled as fascist were neither racist nor utopian. They were rather dictatorial strongman-type governments distinguished by violence and brutality in opposition to both communism and democracy. The association of Nazi-ism with fascism would seem to be the manner in which they both employed gangs of armed thugs to achieve their political ends, the fact that both fascist Italy and Nazi Germany supported

the 1936–39 fascist-like takeover in Spain, and that they aligned as the Axis powers during World War II. In their aggression and oppression, fascist-styled governments were not appreciably different than the communist-styled governments they opposed.
2. Edmund Burke, "An Appeal from the New to the Old Whigs in Consequence of Some Late Discussions in Parliament Relative to the Reflections on the French Revolution," August 1791, *Edmund Burke, Reflections on the Revolution in France and Other Writings*, p. 699. "The people are the natural control on authority; but to exercise and to control together is contradictory and impossible."

Appendix B: Natural Law and Natural Right

1. Kant, "The Critique of Judgment: The Science of Right," *The Critique of Pure Reason, The Critique of Practical Reason and Other Ethical Treatises*, p. 401.
2. Haidt, *The Righteous Mind*, p. 38. Reprinted with permission.
3. The definition of rights has been enlarged to include compulsory benefit schemes, which are not actually rights. Rights and compulsory benefit schemes are two different things. If supplied by government, food, housing, employment, education, and healthcare are compulsory benefit schemes—compulsory, that is, for those who supply the resources. Such schemes empty the public treasury, and the right of property must be taken away from someone else to keep them going. In contrast, the *pursuit* of food, housing, employment, education, and healthcare are rights— rights generalized under the theme *the pursuit of happiness*. Certainly, it is a right to make voluntary contributions toward the end that someone else may receive something but not a right to receive benefits supplied by contributions from others made compulsory by government penalty. Compulsory benefit schemes infringe

on property rights in the form of excess taxation. They also cause dependency in the recipients of the benefits. True rights do not produce dependency, and their exercise does not infringe on the reciprocal rights of everyone else. Of a similar nature are government programs such as Social Security and Medicare. These are sometimes referred to as entitlement programs from which one is entitled to collect benefits after having been compelled to pay into them earlier. The compulsory nature is actually a removal of a right because the ability to choose what you wish to do with your income is taken away. In contrast, voluntary programs permit one to choose to participate or not. If you trust the government to make good on its promises, then you might choose to voluntarily participate in the programs. But to be compelled to participate is a different sort of classification and not a right. Whether such programs and schemes are justified is an entirely different question and one on which there is no comment here. It is only that they should not be misrepresented as rights.

4. In 1948, the United Nations (UN) issued *The Universal Declaration of Human Rights*. The thirty articles it contains were not defended on principles reasoned from human nature or any higher authority; they were simply announced. Thus, there is nothing that would prevent UN ambassadors from declaring a revised set of rights at some later date. Articles 22 and beyond begin to stretch the meaning of rights to include entitlements such as employment, food, housing, and medical care. "Elementary education" declares Article 26 "shall be compulsory" even while parents are supposed to have the right to choose it. Then there are vague though "indispensable" economic, social, and cultural rights, "social services," and entitlement to "a social and international order," which, though perhaps not so intended, are open to interpretation as invitations for government control in pursuit of such easily manipulated goals as "the full development of personality" and "the

maintenance of peace." Most ominous are a number of articles (8, 10, 11, 12, 14, and 29), which contain provisions able to negate the declared rights should they be found contrary to law, contrary to the determinations of a tribunal, or contrary to the purposes and principles of the United Nations, whatever these purposes and principles may be at any given time. These provisions render the document effectively worthless as a source of appeal. Fortunately, the UN's human rights are immaterial to the natural rights of United States citizens, if they would believe it. US citizens' natural rights, being an endowment from their creator, exist whatever the UN might declare.

Appendix C: To What May be Attributed the Increase and Expansion of Christianity?

1. Rodney Stark, *The Triumph of Christianity*; Ehrman, *The Triumph of Christianity*. These histories offer speculative accounts based on how their authors believe religious conversion happens today. Both settle on person-to-person social influence as the cause. A third history, Hill's *Christianity*, follows the same sort of explanatory tone employing such words and phrases as *probably, likely, would have, might have, must have, and we may suppose that* to settle on social influence.
2. Acts 28:22.
3. See Acts 4:1–3, 5:17–18, 6:9–14, 7:54–58, 8:1,3, 9:1–2,23, 12:1–4, 13:50, 14:2,5,19, 17:5–7,13, 18:12, 20:3,19, 21:27–31, and 23:12–15.
4. Rodney Stark, *The Triumph of Christianity*, pp. 174, 299–301; Bart D. Ehrman, *The Triumph of Christianity*, pp. 177, 241.

Bibliography

Adler, Bill, ed., *America's Founding Fathers: Their Uncommon Wisdom and Wit*, Lanham: Taylor Trade Publishing, 2003.

Bailyn, Bernard, *The Ideological Origins of the American Revolution*, Enlarged Edition, Cambridge: Harvard University Press, 1967, 1992.

Brogan, Hugh, *Alexis de Tocqueville, A Life*, New Haven: Yale University Press, 2006.

Burke, Edmund, *Edmund Burke: Selected Writings and Speeches*, Peter J. Stanlis, ed., Washington DC: Regnery Publishing, Inc., 1963.

Burke, Edmund, *Edmund Burke: Reflections on the Revolution in France and Other Writings*, Jesse Norman, ed., New York: Alfred A. Knopf, 2015.

Engdahl, Sylvia, ed., *Amendment XIV: Equal Protection*, Farmington Mills: Greenhaven Press, 2009.

Ehrman, Bart D., *The Triumph of Christianity: How a Forbidden Religion Swept the World*, New York: Simon & Schuster, 2018.

Federer, William J., *America's God and Country Encyclopedia of Quotations*, St. Louis: William J. Federer, 2000.

Fredericks, Carrie, ed., *Amendment XIV: Due Process*, Farmington Mills: Greenhaven Press, 2009.

Guelzo, Allan C., *Lincoln and Douglas: The Debates That Defined America*, New York: Simon & Schuster, 2008.

Guinness, Os, *A Free People's Suicide: Sustainable Freedom and the American Future*, Downers Grove: InterVarsity Press, 2012.

Haidt, Jonathan, *The Righteous Mind: Why Good People Are Divided by Politics and Religion*, New York: Pantheon Book, 2012.

Hill, Jonathan, *Christianity: How a Tiny Sect from a Despised Religion Came to Dominate the Roman Empire*, Minneapolis: Fortress Press, 2010.

Hillsdale College, *The U.S. Constitution: A Reader*, Hillsdale: Hillsdale College Press, 2012.

Himmelfarb, Gertrude, *The Moral Imagination: From Edmund Burke to Lionel Trilling*, Chicago: Ivan R, Dee, 2006.

Holzer, Harold, ed., *The Lincoln-Douglas Debates: The First Complete Unexpurgated Text*, New York: HarperCollins, 1993.

Hume, David, *A Treatise of Human Nature*, First Published 1739-40, London: Penquin Books, 1969.

Jefferson, Thomas, *Thomas Jefferson, Writings*, New York: Literary Classics of the United States, Inc., 1984.

Johannsen, Robert W., ed., *The Lincoln-Douglas Debates of 1858: 150th Anniversary Edition*, New York: Oxford University Press, 2008.

Jones, Dan, *Magna Carta: The Birth of Liberty*, New York: Viking-Penguin Random House LLC, 2015.

Kant, Immanuel, *The Critique of Pure Reason, The Critique of Practical Reason and Other Ethical Treatises*, Chicago: Encyclopedia Britannica, Inc., 1952.

Kitcher, Philip, *Life After Faith: The Case for Secular Humanism*, New Haven: Yale University Press, 2014.

Lehrman, Lewis, E., *Lincoln at Peoria: The Turning Point*, Mechanicsburg: Stackpole Books, 2008.

Lewis, C.S., *Christian Reflections*, Walter Hooper, ed., Grand Rapids: William B. Eerdmans, 1967.

Lewis, C.S., *Mere Christianity*, New York: HarperCollins, 1952, 2001. Lewis, C.S., *Miracles: A Preliminary Study*, New York: HarperCollins, 1947, 2001.

Locke, John, *Second Treatise of Government*, Indianapolis: C.B. Macpherson, ed., Hackett Publishing Co., 1980.

Lutzer, Erwin W., *When a Nation Forgets God: 7 Lessons We Must Learn from Nazi Germany*, Chicago: Moody Publishers, 2010.

Madison, James, *Writings*, New York: Literary Classics of the United States, Inc., 1999.

Pangle, Thomas L., *The Great Debate: Advocates and Opponents of the American Constitution*, Chantilly: The Great Courses, 2007.

Pearcey, Nancy, *Saving Leonardo: A Call to Resist the Secular Assault on Mind, Morals, and Meaning*, Nashville: B&H Publishing Group, 2010.

Robinson, Daniel N., *The Great Ideas of Philosophy, 2nd Edition*, Chantilly: The Great Courses, 2004.

Russell, Bertrand, *A History of Western Philosophy*, New York: Simon & Schuster, 1945, 1972.

Sokal, Alan, *Beyond the Hoax: Science, Philosophy and Culture*, New York: Oxford University Press, 2008.

Sproul, R.C., *The Consequences of Ideas: Understanding the Concepts that Shaped Our World*, Wheaton: Crossway Books, 2000.

Stark, Rodney, *How the West Won: The Neglected Story of the Triumph of Modernity*, Wilmington: Intercollegiate Studies Institute, 2014.

Stark, Rodney, *The Triumph of Christianity: How the Jesus Movement Became the World's Largest Religion*, New York: Harper Collins, 2011.

Stark, Rodney, *The Victory of Reason: How Christianity Led to Freedom, Capitalism, and Western Success*, New York: Random House, 2005.

Whitehead, Alfred North, *Science and the Modern World, Lowell Lectures, 1925*, New York: Macmillan Company, 1925.

Wilson, Jay, *Proof that the Bible Is the Word of God*, Bozeman: 11th Hour Press, 2002.

Zacharias, Ravi, *Deliver Us from Evil*, Dallas: Word Publishing, 1996.

www.ingramcontent.com/pod-product-compliance
Lightning Source LLC
LaVergne TN
LVHW041707070526
838199LV00045B/1248